Wilson Boaventura

Implementing Active Directory consolidated in infrastructures

Wilson Boaventura

Implementing Active Directory consolidated in infrastructures

ScienciaScripts

Imprint

Any brand names and product names mentioned in this book are subject to trademark, brand or patent protection and are trademarks or registered trademarks of their respective holders. The use of brand names, product names, common names, trade names, product descriptions etc. even without a particular marking in this work is in no way to be construed to mean that such names may be regarded as unrestricted in respect of trademark and brand protection legislation and could thus be used by anyone.

Cover image: www.ingimage.com

This book is a translation from the original published under ISBN 978-613-9-65618-9.

Publisher:
Sciencia Scripts
is a trademark of
Dodo Books Indian Ocean Ltd. and OmniScriptum S.R.L publishing group

120 High Road, East Finchley, London, N2 9ED, United Kingdom
Str. Armeneasca 28/1, office 1, Chisinau MD-2012, Republic of Moldova, Europe
Printed at: see last page
ISBN: 978-620-7-79287-0

INDICE

DEDICATORY

I dedicate this work to my children Koriander and Kiesse, my wife Maria Helena, my family in general, and my friends.

THANKS

To Jesus Christ for his guiding light.

To my advisor Eng.^{0} . Joao Paulo for his patience and dedication.

To all the teachers who, directly or indirectly, contributed to increasing my knowledge over these four years, especially to Engineer Leopoldino for his understanding character.

To my colleagues at UTANGA, Ana Cristina, Herlander Sousa, Kiaku, Wilson Katangue, Wilson Paulino, Augusto, Marta Gonga, Ivone Dias, who inspired me to complete this course.

EPILOGUE

No invention has been more beneficial to man than the sky.
Georg Lichtenberg

SUMMARY

0 Active Directory's directory service can be compared to a phone book or a personal organizer. In it we can organize days, weeks, months and even years, recording people's names, birthdays, important data and much more. The directory service has exactly the same meaning, the sense of organizing and above all having a centralized place to search for the information we need in our day-to-day work. The main task to be carried out in this project is the migration from one domain to another in order to bring them together to form part of the same forest of a single domain. With the implementation of this solution, it is hoped that the respective AD Forests and Domains will be consolidated in order to take better advantage of the benefits that a consolidated AD environment brings to organizations, such as the centralized management of network resources in an agile and more secure manner.

Keywords: Active Directory, Migration Tool, DNS, Domain Controller.

INTRODUCTION

Active Directory is everywhere. This is a fact and a challenge for any company that wants to build a unified AD environment. The consolidation of AD domains and forests is the topic most often raised when talking about Active Directory. Commercial organizations, governments and educational organizations are all looking for a more efficient approach to managing their AD and providing AD services to their internal clients (users). However, the complexity of some AD environments is staggering. Many commercial organizations operate more than 10 forests with multiple domains in each forest and a complex network of trust relationships.

There are good reasons for this AD infestation. When AD was launched, it was seen as an extension of the Windows Workgroup and was implemented as a localized, departmental solution. As the years have passed, AD has become a company solution, but many organizations are still managing it as a departmental solution. This architectural legacy keeps many AD administrators employed and allows departments to act as a separate fiefdom within the overall company. While this local autonomy has some benefits, it multiplies the complexity when deploying single ADs which can dramatically increase the cost of implementing new *software* or new work processes in companies.

Kym Gilhooly[1] argues that there is a need to have a clear vision when going for AD consolidation. Many departments implement their own directories to manage servers and workstations, complicating efforts to create a unified structure across the company. To leverage authentication and authorization and manage the benefits that a well-designed AD environment provides, IT managers must control the structures that are organically spreading throughout their companies. It is necessary to carry out a detailed study and assessment, design or redesign and document the entire service directory and identify a management vision. This vision will define what you want an AD to do and guide future decision-making. These decisions determine that the directorate and group policy changes are based on improving efficiency while keeping the network secure.

---

1 Kym Gilhooly in http7/www.statetechma⅜azine.com/article/2013/07/how-consolidate-microsoft-active- directory. Last accessed on 6.12.2016.

OBJECTIVES

General objective

Implement o Active Directory Consolidated (AD consolidation) in network infrastructure with Windows environment at FAO-Luanda headquarters.

Specific objectives

In order to achieve o objective in this project, the following specific objectives were established:

- Analyze the operation of the network infrastructure, services and existing security policies.

- Explain the reason for consolidation and why large companies and organizations are using consolidated forest AD.

- Demonstrate the advantages and disadvantages of consolidated forest AD.

- Design a practical guide for implementing and migrating to consolidated AD for domains and forests.

PROBLEM FORMULATION

The FAO offices in Luandaja have a network infrastructure in a Windows environment with a server running Windows Server 2012 with AD, DNS and DHCP services. In other words, the institution has two (2) separate domains installed and operating in separate physical locations, and there is a connection between them via a VPN. This means that when a user registered in domain "x" moves on a service mission to domain "y", they have to be added as a new user of that domain, assigned new credentials, new types of access, etc., in other words, as if they were from another institution, in addition to the fact that each *site has* to have a person with advanced knowledge of AD or network administration. And in this case, the FAO does not have a post in its institutional organization chart for this purpose, using third parties to do it, implying additional financial costs.

In order to take better advantage of the benefits that a consolidated AD environment can bring, the implementation of this solution is proposed.

BACKGROUND

There are real benefits to be found in a consolidated Active Directory (AD) environment. A shared AD infrastructure allows for user mobility, common user configuration processes, consolidated reporting, unified machine management, etc.

Every IT administrator faces a series of Active Directory management challenges that include managing user accounts in Active Directory almost every day. Configuring user properties manually is extremely time-consuming, tiresome and error-prone, especially in a large and complex Windows network. AD managers and IT administrators often have to perform repetitive and trivial tasks, which often end up draining their free time and even decreasing productivity. What's more, performing these tasks using native tools such as PowerShell also requires a deeper knowledge of AD management and related technologies, and even then it's not without its problems and complexities.

In the proposed work we are going to go into detail about consolidating data from various sources in a centralized environment. We will obtain *inputs* from small and large offices to find out the difference in the impact caused by implementing or migrating consolidated AD because the network architecture and hardware in each office will depend on its size.

WORK STRUCTURE AND ORGANIZATION

This work is organized as follows:

• Chapter 1 describes the theoretical foundation, i.e. those theories already studied that will lead us to an understanding of what we intend to implement and improve the elaboration of our work.

• Chapter 2 describes the methods, techniques and tools used to carry out the work. This chapter also describes the field of study and analyzes the procedures used to carry out this work.

• Chapter 3 presents the results of the analysis carried out in the previous chapter. It is dedicated to the system's architecture. It contains all the technologies, design standards and methodologies used to implement the project. This section also presents the proposed diagrams and the basic configuration.

• Finally, we present the conclusions drawn from the project. This final chapter also presents suggestions and recommendations for good practices before migrating or consolidating an AD.

CHAPTER 1 - THEORETICAL BACKGROUND

In this chapter we'll cover some concepts about computer networks, architecture and existing network types to help us understand how best to implement our project. Also in this chapter we will talk about issues such as Active Directory, DNS, DHCP and Organizational Units, which is the fundamental part of our project.

1.1- Computer Networks

1.1.2- Definition

In general terms, a network is a set of systems or objects linked together. Similarly, a computer network is made up of two or more computers linked together in such a way that they can share resources, data and programs (*Gouveia & Magalhães, 2013*).

Even in environments that are not computer-related, but make use of computers, the use of networks can be easily evidenced. Networks are not a new technology. They have existed since the time of the first computers, but the evolution of technology has allowed computers to communicate better at a lower cost.

Computer networks arose from the need to exchange information, where it is possible to access data that is physically located far away from us, such as in banking systems. In this type of system, we have our account data stored somewhere, it doesn't matter where, but whenever we need to consult information about it, we just need to access an ATM or even without leaving our home or office via the *internet banking* service provided by the bank itself. In addition to the advantage of exchanging data, there is also the advantage of sharing peripherals, which can mean a reduction in equipment costs. The figure below shows a local network with printer sharing (peripheral) that can be used by 3 desktop computers (PC) and a laptop.

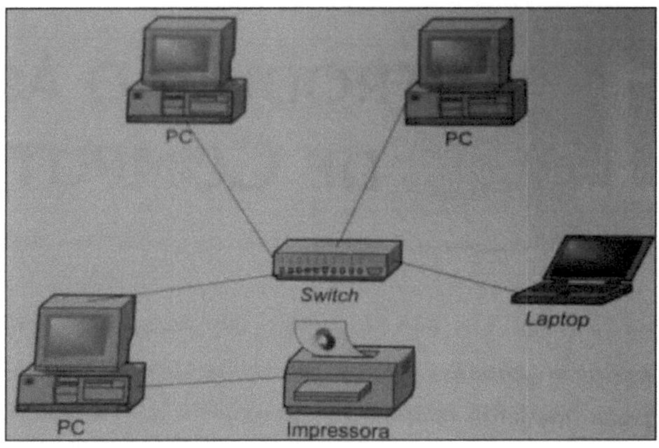

Figure 1.1 Local Area Network with Sharing

Source: Gouveia & Magalhaes, 2013

It's important to know that when we refer to data, we don't just mean files, but any type of information that can be obtained from a computer. The main reasons for setting up a computer network are:

> Enable the sharing of information (programs and data) stored on network computers;

> Allow the sharing of resources associated with interconnected machines;

> Allow information to be exchanged between computers;

> Enable the exchange of information between computer users;

> Enable the use of remotely located computers;

> Centralized management of resources and data;

> Improve the security of Shared data and resources.

1.1.3- Data transmission on a network

Computer networks facilitate the transmission of data. This data is sent over the network via channels that operate in three transmission modes, which we describe below:

Simplex: in this type of transmission there are two types of device, the transmitter - called Tx and the receiver - called Rx; their roles will never be reversed, i.e. the transmitter can only transmit and never receive, while the receiver can only receive and never transmit. In other words, transmission only takes place in one direction.

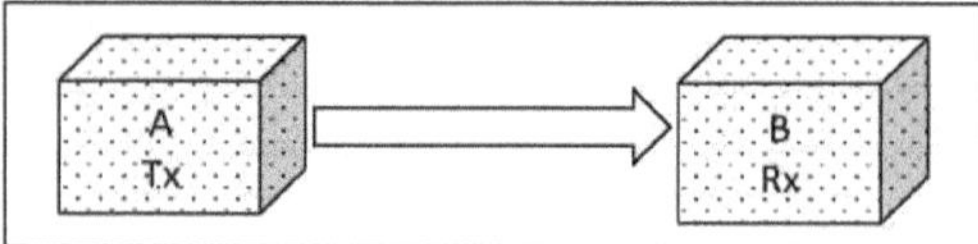

Figure 1.2 Simplex transmission

Source: Gouveia & Magalhaes, 2013

Half-Duplex: this is a type of bidirectional transmission, but as they share the same transmission medium, it is not possible to transmit and receive at the same time. Traditionally, transmission on networks follows this pattern.

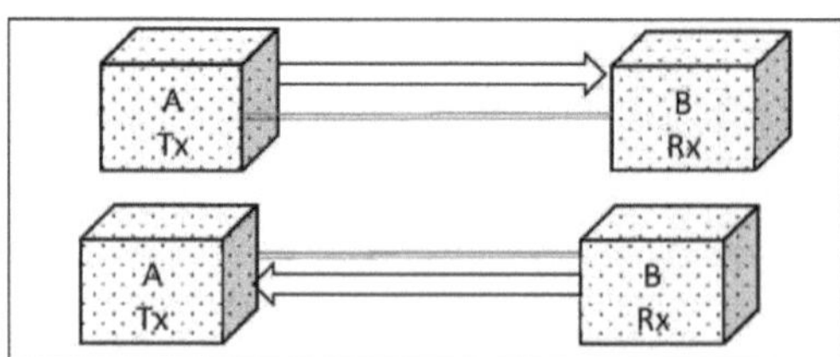

Figure 1.3 Half-Duplex Transmission

Source: Gouveia & Magalhaes, 2013

Full-Duplex: this is true bidirectional communication, where the transmitter can receive data from another computer during its transmission.

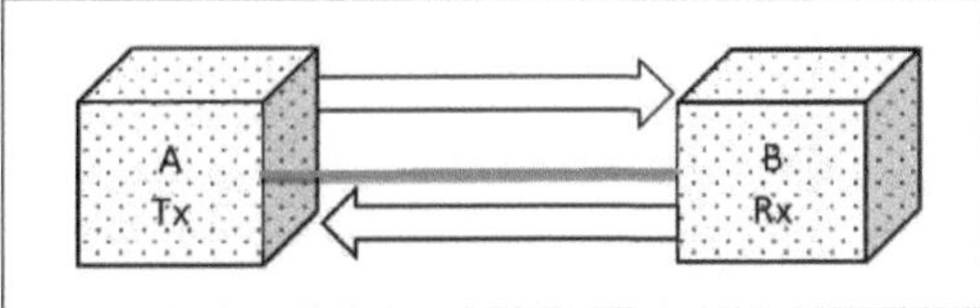

Figure 1.4 Full-Duplex Transmission

Source: Gouveia & Magalhaes, 2013

1.2- Types of networks

The purpose of a computer network is to share resources. From the point of view of how the data on a network is shared, we can classify networks into two basic types depending on the architecture of the network's operating system:

> Point-to-point: used in small networks;

> Client/server: which can be used in small networks or large networks.

This type of classification does not depend on the physical structure used by the network (the way it is set up), but rather on the way it is configured in *software*, as mentioned in the previous paragraph.

1.1.1- Point-to-Point Networks

This is the simplest type of network that can be set up, and practically all operating systems come with support for point-to-point networking (with the exception of DOS). In this type of network, data and peripherals can be shared without much bureaucracy, any PC can easily read and write files stored on other PCs and also use the peripherals installed on other PCs, but this will only be possible if there is a correct configuration, which is done on each PC. In other words, there is no one PC that has the role of network server, everyone can be a data or peripheral server.

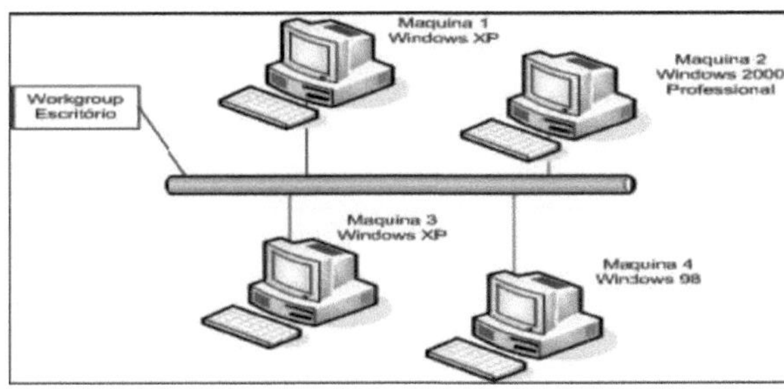

Figure 1.5 Point-to-point network

Source: http://cefiosil011.wikidot.com/icorli-david

Although it is possible to load programs stored on other PCs, it is preferable for all programs to be installed individually on each PC.

1.1.1.1- Advantages and disadvantages of a peer-to-peer network

1.1.1.1.1- Advantages

> Used in small networks (usually up to ten PCs);

> Low cost;

> Easy to implement;

> Simple cabling system;

1.1.1.1.2- Disadvantages:

> Low security;

> Micros work normally without being connected to the network;

> Micros installed in the same work environment;

> There is no network administrator;

> There are no microservers;

> The network will have problems growing in size.

1.1.2- Client-Server Networks

This type of network is used when you want to connect more than 10 computers or when you want to have greater network security. This type of network features a **server** and a **client**. The server is a computer that offers specialized resources to the other PCs on the network, i.e. in client/server network architecture, the services are located on a dedicated computer (server) whose function is to respond to requests from workstations (clients). It is on the server that the services needed to run the network reside. Although both machines are PCs with the same basic architecture, client and server computers usually have different hardware and software configurations. The server is usually a more powerful, complex and expensive machine than a simple PC and should also have a more powerful and expensive Operating System (OS) than the OS installed on a PC (Gouveia & Magalhaes, 2013).

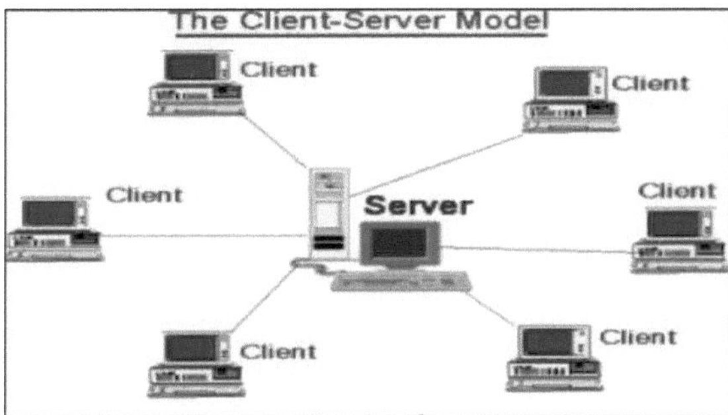

Figure 1.6 ClientZServer network

Source:cefiosil011.wikidot.com/icorli-david/2014

The great advantage of having a dedicated server is the speed with which it responds to client requests. This is because, as well as being specialized in the task in question, it doesn't normally perform other tasks. In networks where performance is not an important factor, you can have non-dedicated servers, i.e. server PCs that are also used as workstations.

Another advantage of client/server networks is the centralized administration and configuration, which improves network security and organization.

For a client/server network, we can have several types of dedicated servers that will vary according to the needs of the network, below are examples of server types:

File Server: this is a server responsible for storing data files - such as text files, spreadsheets, etc. It is important to know that this server is only responsible for delivering the data to the requesting user (client), no processing takes place on this server, the programs responsible for processing the file data must be installed on the client computers.

Print Server: this is a server responsible for processing print requests from PCs on the network and sending them to the available printers. The server is responsible for managing the printing.

Application Server: is responsible for running client/server applications such as a database. Unlike file servers, this type of server processes information.

Mail server: responsible for processing and delivering electronic messages. If the e-mail is intended for someone outside the network, it must be passed on to the communication server.

Proxy server: used to communicate your local network with other networks, such as the Internet. If you access the Internet via a conventional telephone line, the communication server can be a computer with a MODEM card. It ensures that all data transmission between you and the Internet is authorized.

1.1.2.1- Advantages and Disadvantages of a Client-Server Network

1.1.2.1.1- Advantages

> Normally used in networks with more than 10 computers or small networks that need a high degree of security;

> Higher performance than point-to-point networks;

> High network security and organization;

> Network configuration and maintenance is done centrally;

> High speed of response to customer requests;

1.1.2.1.2- Disadvantages

> Higher cost than point-to-point networks;

> Implementation requires specialists;

> Single point of failure, without an operational server the network doesn't work.

1.3- Components of a network

In a computer network environment, there are several elements that make up the network - both in physical and logical terms - connected to each other, allowing us to take advantage of all the network's potential. It is important at this point to have an overview of these elements that characterize a network environment.

1.3.1- Physical media

Most networks establish communication through a physical medium, be it copper wire or fiber optic wire, despite the growth of *wireless* networks. The three main types of network cable used are o **coaxial cable**, o **twisted pair cable** and o **fiber optic cable**. There's also the **network card,** which is the interface that connects the computer to the network. This device facilitates the physical, electrical and electronic connection to the network cable. When choosing a network card, we must take into account its speed, the type of connection according to the network topology, e.g. RJ-45 for twisted pair cable or BNC for coaxial cable; the type of interface with the computer e.g. ISA, PCI or PCMCIA for laptops.

1.3.1.1- Switch

The **Switch** is used to connect the various devices on the network into various segments. It establishes a direct connection between the transmitting device and the receiving device.

1.3.1.2- Router

It is a device that connects several normally different segments of a network into a single internetwork. Its function is to get data to its destination based on the information it obtains from the network itself.

The **gateway** connects different network environments and is a combination of hardware and software. It is usually called an outgoing gateway (also an incoming gateway) because it allows data to flow out and in, as is the case with using the Internet and e-mail.

1.3.1.4- Firewall

The **Firewal** currently also has the functionality of a Gateway, but its primary characteristic is to serve as a network protector against illegal entries and/or unsolicited communications between computers on the network. It should be noted that a *firewall* can also be a software application.

1.3.1.5- Customer

It corresponds to any computer that seeks to use Shared resources or access information that is located at Centralized points on the network.

1.3.1.6- Server

It corresponds to a computer that centralizes the provision of Shared resources or information and that responds to requests from client computers on the network.

1.3.1.7- MODEM

It is the device that allows data to be transferred from computer to computer, for example the Internet connection via a telephone line. It corresponds to an analog or digital telephone medium, so the connection interface is called a MODEM because it is responsible for a process called modulation and demodulation.

1.3.2- Yogic Media

1.3.2.1- Network operating system

For a computer to operate on a network in the role of both client and server, the operating system installed on the computer must be able to support network communication operations. All current operating systems support and recognize network operation, implementing the functions of using them as clients and servers in their input and output operations.

1.3.2.2- Protocol

It corresponds to a communication standard that exists on a network. In order for two computers to exchange information, they must use the same network protocol.

1.3.2.3- Topology

It corresponds to the logical design of a network, showing mainly the path of communication between the computers on the network.

1.4- Classification of computer networks

Computer networks can be classified in two ways: by their geographical dispersion and by their interconnection topology. In terms of their geographical dispersion, they can be classified as:

1.4.2- Local Area Network (LAN)

LANs, as they are also called, are small geographically dispersed networks, located in the same physical space such as a room, building or campus, with the purpose of sharing resources associated with computers, or allowing communication between users of these devices.

The first local networks were limited to a distance of 180 m (from a central office to the furthest office) and a maximum of 30 computers. With current technology, these limitations have been overcome, however, for reasons of ease of network administration, it is necessary to subdivide them into small logical areas called "workgroups" (Gouveia & Magalhâes, 2013).

With the advent of Active Directory, managing the network and these workgroups is even easier, as we'll see below.

1.4.3- Metropolitan Area Network (MAN)

They are used to interconnect dispersed computers in a wider geographical area such as a city, where it is not possible to interconnect them using local area network technology.

"MANs are actually a set of several LANs connected via MODEMs or routers, with the connection made via telephone line, cable or even wireless connection." (Gouveia & Magalhdes, 2013). "

1.4.4- Wide Area Networks (WAN)

It is used to interconnect computers located in different cities, states or countries. A WAN is a remote access network that connects local computers over long distances. Companies that expand their offices to distant geographical locations take advantage of WANs because they bring them enormous benefits such as sharing data and resources even without being in the same physical space. As mentioned earlier, we can interconnect networks so that a different network can communicate with and use the resources of another network. Among the forms of interconnection between networks, we highlight the Internet, Extranet and Intranet.

1.5- The Internet

The Internet - known as the World Wide Web - is a global system of interconnected computer networks that use their own set of protocols (TCP/IP) to serve users in the exchange of information and use of resources. It is a network of several other networks, made up of millions of private and public companies, governments and schools with a local and global reach and which is connected to a wide variety of wireless and optical electronic network technologies. The Internet brings an extensive range of information resources and services such as the World Wide Web (WWW) and e-mail services, for example.

1.6- The Intranet

The Intranet is a network created for processing information in a company or organization. Its use includes services such as *software* and document distribution, database access and training. The intranet has this name because it usually employs applications associated with the Internet, such as web pages, web browsers, FTP *sites,* email, newsgroups and distribution lists, accessible only to people who are part of the organization.

The use of one or more routers can allow the internal network to interact with the Internet. It uses TCP/IP, HTTP and other Internet protocols for communications and is characterized by the use of WWW technology within a corporate network.

1.7- The Extranet

It is a private (corporate) network that uses Internet protocols and the services of telecommunications providers to share some of its information with suppliers, vendors, partners and consumers.

It can be seen as the part of an Intranet that is extended to users outside the company. Security and privacy are key aspects to allow external access, which is normally carried out via WWW interfaces, with authentication, encryption and access restrictions. It can be used to exchange large volumes of data, share information between vendors, work cooperatively between companies, etc.

1.8- Virtual Private Network

Virtual Private Network (VPN) is a network for the exclusive use of users authorized by a company to connect to the Internet from anywhere in the world. A VPN works like a private network, except that it carries data over the infrastructure of the public data network or the Internet itself.

Boavida, Bemardes and Vapi in their book "Administração de Redes Informations" 2011, state that a VPN should be considered as a communications environment with restricted access to a specific community, built on a shared communications medium. VPNs not only allow remote users access to the internal network, but are a means of extending the network to geographically remote locations such as branch offices or any other facility of varying size.

1.9- Wireless networks

Technology today has reached a degree of dissemination in society that makes it present in all areas of work and even in the area of entertainment. This growth has meant that people need to connect to networks anywhere, anytime. In many situations it is impossible or even very expensive to set up a connection structure using conventional cabling. That's where wireless networking comes in. Wireless networks (also known as Wireless and WiFi) are infrastructures that allow computers to connect to each other or to a conventional network, using communication technologies that dispense with the use of cables, such as radio waves.

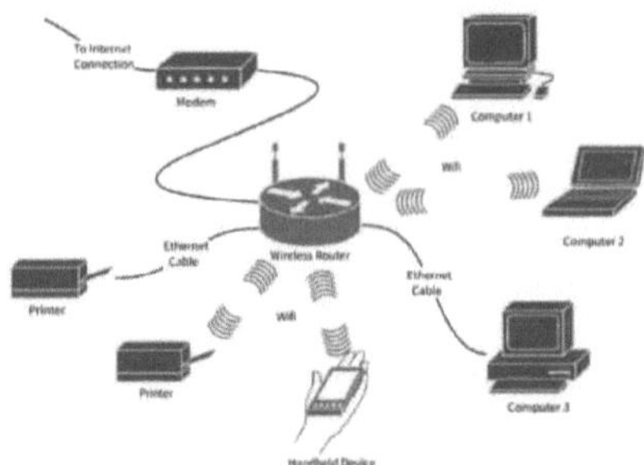

Figure 1.7 Wireless networks

Source: lucidchart.com

The main objectives of local wireless network technologies in general, and IEEE 802.11 technology in particular, are to provide high-speed communication capabilities in relatively restricted geographical areas, such as homes, schools, warehouses, airports, etc. (Boavida, Bernardes and Vapi 2011).

The great advantage of wireless networking is the mobility it gives computers, particularly notebooks and handhelds (palmtops or PDAs).

1.10- Network topologies

Layout is a term for the way physical objects are organized in a particular place. A *layout* can be a drawing, map or diagram of objects arranged in a certain way.

"The physical topology of the network describes the layout of the cables, computers and all the components of the network." (Gouveia & Magalhdes, 2013). "

The way computers are connected in a network can make them more efficient in their networking activities. The topology of a network can affect its performance and capacity.

Setting up or organizing a network is not a simple process. You have to combine different types of components, choose the network operating system, as well as planning how these components will be connected in different types of environments. At this point, the topology of the network is crucial, because it defines how these components will be interconnected in different environments and situations and ultimately defines how information will propagate on the network. The physical topology of the network will also define the logical topology of the network or, as it is more commonly known, the network technology to be used.

The most common basic topology structures that make up a network are: Bus, Ring, Star and Mesh.

1.10.1- Bus Topology (BUS)

In the bus topology, the computers are connected to a single segment called the central bus or backbone. This segment connects all the computers in that segment on a single line. Communication is broadcast, data is sent to the bus and all computers see this data, however, it will only be received by the recipient (Gouveia &

Magalhàes, 2013).

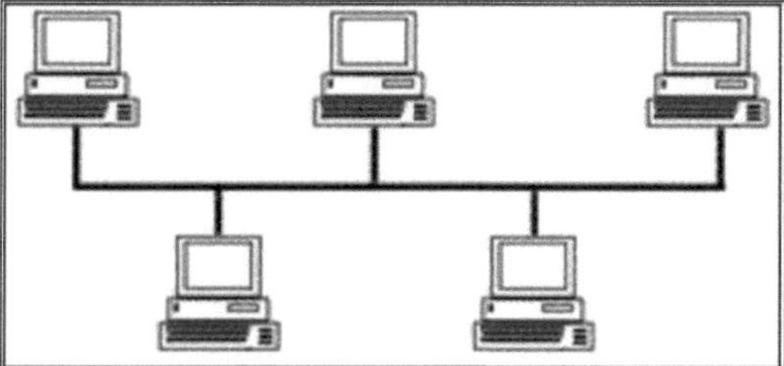

Figure 1.8 Bus topology

Source: computerhope.com

There are some problems that can cause a network with a bus topology to no longer be operational. These problems are:

Faulty or loose terminal: if a terminal is faulty, loose, or not present at all, the electrical signals will be returned on the cable, causing the other computers to be unable to send data.

Break in the **_backbone_**: when a break occurs in the _backbone_, the ends at the break point will not be terminated and the signals will start to return in the cable, causing the network to shut down. The break is sometimes not visible and is internal to the cable, making it difficult to identify.

Adding or removing computers: when adding or removing a new computer, it may be necessary to disconnect a connector in order to add another connector or remove the first one. In this case, the cable momentarily runs out of ends at the connection point, causing the entire network to come to a standstill until it is reconnected.

The bus topology was a pioneer in Ethernet topologies, but it has fallen into disuse as a network topology because of the problems it presents and also because of the low speed of coaxial cable compared to technologies that use twisted pair or fiber optic cable.

1.10.2- Star Topology

In the star topology, the computers are connected to a central point which has the function of distributing the signal sent by one of the computers to all the others connected to this central point, which can be a hub or a switch. This topology is so called because its design resembles a star.

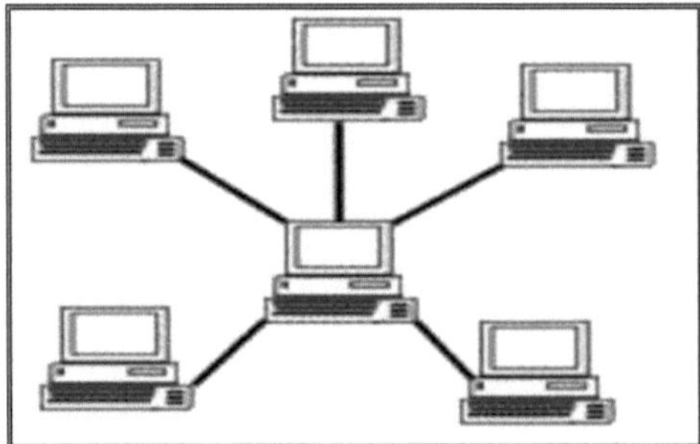

Figure 1.9 Star topology

Source: computerhope.com

The problems or disadvantages of using this topology can be summarized as follows:

Using a large number and length of cables: in large network installations you will need a cable to connect each computer to the hub. Depending on how far the hub is from the computers, the length and quantity of cables can become significant.

Loss of connection if the central node (switch) fails: if, for any reason, the switch is deactivated or fails, all the computers connected to this switch will lose connection with each other.

The main advantages of using the star topology over the previous topology are:

Central monitoring: LEDs on the hub indicate whether a network segment is active or not. If a light goes out, you can immediately find out which computer on the network is disabled. These LEDs also indicate how much the network is being used.

Break isolation: If one of the cables breaks, only the computer connected to that cable will be disabled. The rest of the network will not be affected.

Easy maintenance of computers: Connecting a computer to the network is very simple, just plug a new cable into the switch and the connection is up and running.

The star topology is the most widely used today, due to its ease of maintenance and low cost, as well as having the most modern technologies that allow for good traffic speeds. The variations in the implementation of this topology basically involve the use of other devices at the central point, such as *switches*, and also other more modern cabling such as optical fiber.

1.10.3- Ring Topology

In a ring topology, computers are connected in a ring structure or to each other in a closed circuit. Communication is one-way from computer to computer. An important feature of this topology is that each computer receives the communication from the previous computer and relays it to the next computer if the information is not intended for it. Communication between computers is done through a process called token or baton passing. A special signal called a token (baton) circulates around the ring "clockwise" and only when it receives the *token* does a computer transmit its signal.

The signal travels around the ring until it reaches its destination, passing through all the other computers. Only after receiving the signal back does the computer release the *token,* allowing another computer to communicate.

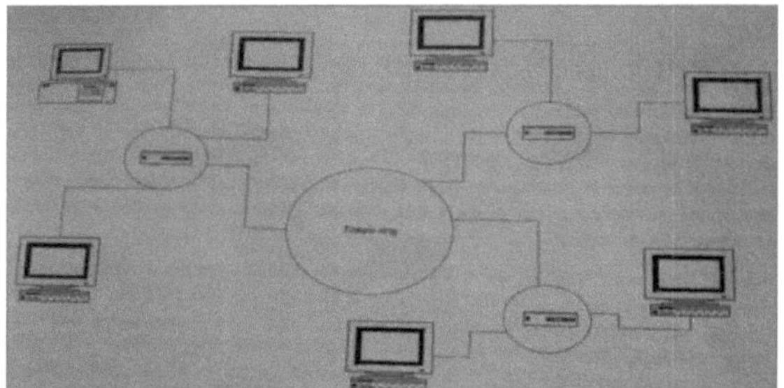

Figure 1.10 Ring Topology

Source: Gouveia & Magalhaes, 2013

The pure implementation of this topology is not used, as it would require each computer to be always on and transmitting to the next in the ring sequence. The most common implementation found is that used by the most modern Token-ring networks, which use a central device called a MAU (Multi Access Unit) that allows the network to be subdivided.

The main advantages of the ring topology are as follows:

-   Short cable length.

-   No cable cabinets are needed. The connections are made at each node.

-   The wiring design is quite simple.

The main disadvantages of the ring topology are as follows:

-   The failure of one node causes the entire network to fail.

-   Difficulty in locating faults (the failure of one node causes the failure of all the others).

-   The difficulty in reconfiguring the network.

-   Difficulty in establishing a network access protocol, since each node will have to ensure the continuity of information and will only then be able to send its own information after certifying that the network is available.

The ring topology implemented in LANs is falling into disuse, mainly because of the low transmission rates.

1.10.4- Mesh Topology

In the mesh topology, computers are connected physically and directly between each node (everyone communicates with everyone else), forming a mesh-like design. Although rarely used in local networks, a variant of this topology - the hybrid mesh - is used on the Internet and in some WANs, thus creating alternative routes for connecting networks.

The main advantages of the mesh topology are the existence of alternative communication paths between two points in the network and fault tolerance.

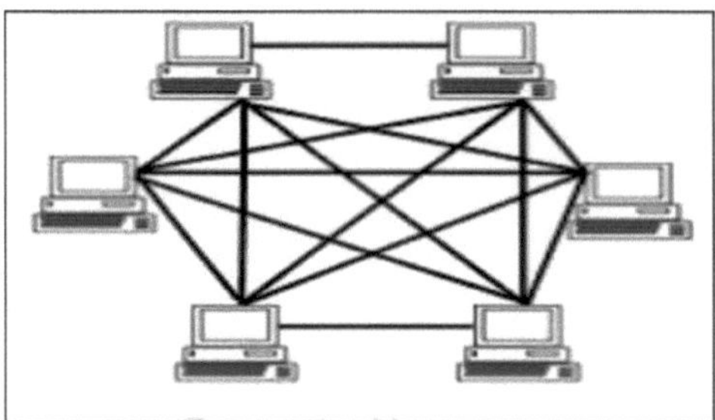

Figure 1.11 Mesh Topology

Source: computerhope.com

1.11- 0 TCP/IP

TCP/IP is a set of protocols that allow computers to interconnect (*Gouveia & Magalhães, Redes de Computadores 2013*).

TCP/IP (Transmission Control Protocol/Internet Protocol) is not just one protocol, but a suite or group of protocols that has become an industry standard for providing communication in heterogeneous environments, such as UNIX, Windows, MAC OS, minicomputers and even *mainframes*. Today o TCP/IP refers to a suite of protocols used on the Internet. This standard set of protocols specifies how computers communicate and provides the conventions for the connection and routes to be used by any packet or flow of packets.

TCP/IP has always been considered a rather heavy protocol, requiring a lot of memory and hardware to use. With the development of graphical interfaces, the evolution of processors and the efforts of operating system developers to offer TCP/IP for their platforms with performance equal to or sometimes superior to other protocols, TCP/IP has become an indispensable protocol because most LANs require its use for access to the outside world. TCP/IP offers a number of benefits, including:

> **Standardization:** a standard, routable protocol that is the most complete and acceptable protocol available today. All modern operating systems support TCP/IP and most large networks rely on TCP/IP for the majority of their traffic.

> **Interconnectivity**: a **technology for connecting non-similar systems**. Many standard Connectivity Utilities are available to access and transfer data between these non-similar systems, including FTP (File Transfer Protocol) and Telnet (Terminal Emulation Protocol).

>   **Routing:** allows and enables older and newer technologies to connect to the Internet. Works with line protocols such as PPP (Point to Point Protocol) allowing remote connection from dial-up or dedicated lines. Works with the IPC mechanisms and interfaces most commonly used by operating systems, such as Windows Sockets and NetBIOS.

>   **A robust**, scalable, cross-platform **protocol** with a structure for use on **client/server** operating systems, allowing applications of this size to be used between two distant points.

>   **Internet:** It is through the TCP/IP protocol suite that we gain access to the Internet. Local networks distribute Internet access servers (proxy servers) and local hosts connect to these servers to gain access to the Internet. This access can only be achieved if the switches are configured to use TCP/IP.

In TCP/IP, in addition to the physical address, there are two other levels of addressing: Domain Names and IP Addresses. Domain names are used in a TCP/IP environment through a service called DNS, Domain Name Server.

DNS provides a hierarchical naming scheme for TCP/IP hosts. This scheme allows organizations to logically divide their networks and delegate authority to network administrators in each area. These divisions are called "authority zones".

The domain name has been standardized as the naming structure on the Internet. The domain name has the following characteristics:

>   Set of names in a domain hierarchy.

>   Names are separated by periods.

>   The domain name is limited to 256 characters.

>   The names are read from right to left, starting at the root.

We'll cover DNS in a specific chapter later.

1.11.1- O TCP/IP its Layers and Protocols

0 TCP/IP is made up of a series of standard protocols, designed to allow connections between subnets and even networks from different providers. Although TCP/IP is associated with the OSI model, it uses only four layers: the Link Layer, the Internet Layer, the Transport Layer and the Application Layer.

1.11.1.1- Link Layer

The Link Layer (also called the network interface layer) is the lowest level layer in the model. It is responsible for placing and removing frames (packets) on the physical medium. This layer contains the protocols used in the various physical network communication technologies. These protocols are not actually part of the TCP/IP suite, but rather allow a TCP/IP host to communicate with other hosts on the network.

The Link Layer is where it is defined how the information will be transported on the network, say Gouveia &

Magalhaes, in Redes de Computadores 2013.

1.11.1.2- Internet Layer

The Internet layer is responsible for addressing, packaging and routing functions. Three protocols are defined at this layer:

1.11.1.2.1- IP

(Internet Protocol) is responsible for addressing and routing packets between sender and receiver so that information doesn't get lost on the network. It and TCP are the most important protocols in the whole set.

1.11.1.2.2- ARP

(Address Resolution Protocol) establishes a link between the physical address of the network card and the IP address.

1.11.1.2.3- ICMP

(Internet Control Message Protocol) is responsible for sending messages and reporting errors related to the delivery of a packet. In this way, an ICMP message is sent and the packet of information not received is sent again.

The Internet Group Management Protocol is responsible for managing the information that circulates on the Internet and Intranet using the TCP/IP protocol.

1.11.1.3- Transport Layer

The transport layer is responsible for communication between two hosts. There are two protocols in this layer.

1.11.1.3.1- TCP

Transmission Control Protocol allows you to secure the transfer of information (connection-oriented) and check that it has been received by the receiving computer (acknowledgment). If not, it sends the information again.

1.11.1.3.2- UDP

User Datagram Protocol is responsible for providing connectionless communication and does not guarantee the delivery of packets. Applications using UDP typically transfer small amounts of data at a time. Reliable delivery is the responsibility of the application. UDP does not perform packet *acknowledgment*. It simply connects and sends the data, which makes it faster but less efficient.

1.11.1.4- Application Layer

It is through this that applications gain access to the network. It uses the following protocols: HTPP, SMTP, FTP and SNMP.

1.11.1.4.1- HTTP

Hyper Text Transport Protocol is the protocol used to control communication between the Internet server and the browser. When you open an Internet page, you see text, images, *links* or other services linked to the Internet or an Intranet. HTTP is responsible for redirecting services when we select one of the options on the web page.

1.11.1.4.2- SMTP

The Simple Mail Transfer Protocol is used to transfer e-mails between servers. The email server uses the POP (Post Office Protocol) or IMAP (Internet Mail Access Protocol) service to send emails to users.

1.11.1.4.3- FTP

File Transfer Protocol, this protocol allows the transfer of data or files between computers even with different operating systems such as Linux and Windows. FTP is also a command that allows a client to connect to an FTP server in order to transfer data via the Internet or Intranet.

1.11.1.4.4- SNMP

The Simple Network Management Protocol is a communication protocol that collects information about all the components in the network, such as switches, routers, bridges and the computers connected to the network.

The TCP/IP package distributes protocols between the four layers. This distribution provides a standardized set of protocols so that computers can communicate with each other.

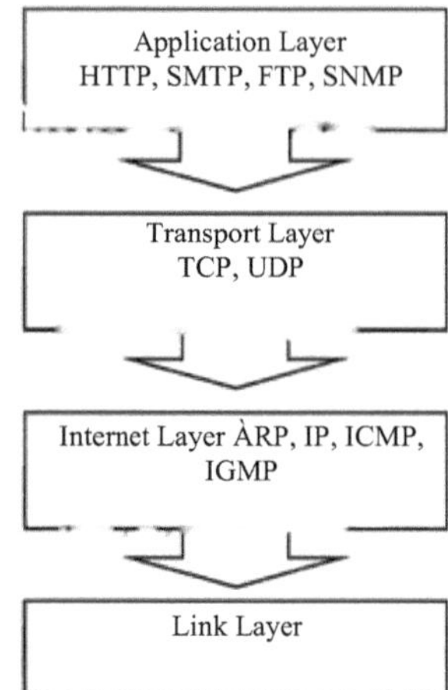

Figure 1.12 TCP/IP Layers and their Protocols

Source: Gouveia & Magalhaes, Computer Networks 2013

1.12- DNS

Now we're going to talk about DNS (Domain Name System), what it is and how it works. We'll also look at some security aspects involving DNS.

Boavida, Bemardes and Vapi in "Administraçâo de Redes Informâticas" 2011, consider DNS to be the most critical service on the Internet, because all the others - e-mail, WWW, FTP, etc. - depend on its effective operation. Its main objective is to convert computer names into IP addresses. In this context, DNS is a fundamental support service, which is why it is the service whose implementation is considered first when designing a network or connecting an isolated network to the Internet.

The main function of DNS, as we mentioned above, is to convert names into IP addresses and vice versa, store this information and share it. Computers, and not only computers, on the network are identified by IP addresses and not by names. When we type in the FAO address (www.fao.org), for example, we are actually accessing a machine that will have a specific IP address on the Internet. The DNS server will try to find out which address corresponds to which name. It will forward the request to another DNS server and if it doesn't find it either, it will forward it to another one and so on until the IP address is found.

1.12.1- How DNS works

According to Boavida, Bernardes and Vapi, 2011[2] DNS is a distributed database containing mapping information between domain names and information relating to those domains. It is also an application protocol that allows communication between clients (which request, for example, the conversion of a name

---

2 Boavida, Bernardes and Vapi "Administraçâo deRedesInformâticas" 2aed.pag. 118, FCA 2011.

into one or more addresses) and servers (which respond with the available information). DNS defines the process of interrogation and updating between servers and the organization of the information in the database.

Like most Internet services, DNS is based on the client-server model. A request for information from the DNS is called a query. For a client computer to query a server, it needs a resolver, a set of routines or processes that a user application uses to translate the name into an IP address and which is the real client of the service.

1.12.2- Domain name space

It is important to describe the DNS as a repository of information that contains all the correspondences between names and IP addresses of all the computers on the Internet - the Domain Name Space. As well as a communication protocol between clients and name servers, DNS also provides a naming space where each device on the network is associated with a unique name. This name can be used by users and applications to identify the device as an alternative to its IP address, says Boavida, Bernardes and Vapi, 2011[3] .

This namespace is a vast and important repository of information that defines all the correspondences between names and addresses of devices accessible on the Internet. Each domain has a unique name, depending on its position in the tree. The Fully Qualified Domain Name (FQDN) of a computer includes the name of the computer and the names of all the Subdomains up to the root separated by quotation marks ("").

1.12.3- Zones and Domains

Zone is a hierarchical collection of Domain Names, the root of which has been delegated to one or more servers. Desmond, B. Active Directory, 2013.

For example, let's assume that the Domain ao.fao.org has been delegated to the server named DCLAD.fao.org, all the Domain Names contained under fao.org that DCLAD.fao.org had been delegated authority over will be considered part of the fao.org Zone.

1.12.4- Security

If security is a fundamental aspect in the implementation of any service, in the case of DNS it is even more relevant given its role as an infrastructure service on which additional Internet services depend.

1.12.4.1- Access Control List (ACL)

These are lists of permissions that objects have for network resources. It also works as a firewall in a router to determine which computers are using the router. An ACL associates a name with a list of one or more addresses.

---

3 Boavida, Bernardes and Vapi "Administraçào de Redes Informdticas" 2aed.pag. 120,121, FCA 2011.

1.13- ODHCP

When it comes to assigning addresses in a LAN, IP address management is a crucial aspect, since IP addresses are indispensable for identifying the originators and recipients of data units and are therefore essential for communication to be possible. In local networks, there are basically two alternatives for assigning addresses, which we'll look at below. The DHCP service aims to reduce the complexity and time-consuming nature of TCP/IP configurations on a network (Boavida, Bernardes and Vapi, 2011).

Address allocation is a critical task because it must be done in a way that prevents duplicate addresses from existing on a global scale. In wide area networks or backbone networks, it is relatively easy to manage address allocation given the infrequency with which the equipment and topologies of these networks are changed. In local area networks, however, where there may be hundreds of users, many of whom are temporary or mobile users, address allocation and management can be complex and must be carried out efficiently. In local networks, IP addresses can be assigned in two ways: manual configuration and automatic or dynamic configuration. Both have advantages and disadvantages, but it is up to the network administrator to decide on the best distribution scheme.

Manual configuration has the advantage of simplicity. On a small network, with users staying on for long periods of time, it is enough for the administrator to keep a record of the addressing plan and IP assignments. This avoids spending money on specialized hardware and software.

The **automatic** or dynamic **configuration** for IPv4 is DHCP (Dynamic Host Configuration Protocol). DHCP assigns clients an IP address selected from a predefined range of addresses called a scope. This type of service greatly facilitates the work of the network system administrator, who no longer has to worry about assigning all the network addresses.

1.14- Active Directory

When Microsoft introduced Active Directory (AD) in Windows 2000 Server, it caused an evolution in the field of directory services at operating system level. After its birth, AD took the lead in directory services, using LDAP as a base and communication through replication, it launched various features and, above all, tools to facilitate information management in companies. At this point, we're going to see why this service known as AD is so important in the lives of small, medium and large companies, and outline the logical and physical topology of Active Directory in very simple concepts.

As we saw above, AD appears in MS Windows 2000 Server as a directory service solution capable of responding to the requirements of organizations of various sizes. It aims to provide a central point for managing various network resources such as user accounts, computers, applications, printers and policies.

According to Microsoft (How Active Directory Searches Work, 2010), Active Directory is a domain control technology traditionally implemented by the company in Windows operating systems, based essentially on the company's customization of the LDAP protocol. AD makes use of the Lightweight Directory Access Protocol (LDAP) version 2 and 3, Microsoft's implementation of Kerberos, the DNS service and concepts similar to X.500 directories and Organizational Units (OU) are also used.

AD is a Domain Controller that authenticates and authorizes all users and computers on a Windows domain-type network, assigns and enforces security policies for all authenticated computers, such as software installation and updates. AD is used in companies with Windows networks, where network administrators have chosen to use this feature as a way of centralizing the administration of resources as well as security. As a facility, it centrally stores user and computer data, allowing users to have just one password to access all the resources available on the network.

1.14.1- The Directory Service

A directory service is a hierarchical information source that contains data about users, files and other network objects (A. Rosa, *2012*).

The directory service includes a set of rules called Schema that defines the object classes and attributes that can be stored in AD. The directory can also be used to share files, printers and manage workstation updates via WSUS (Windows Server Update Services), all in a simple, manageable console.

1.14.2- The Global Catalog

An important concept when we talk about AD is the Global Catalog. The server that has the Global Catalog (GC) is called the Global Catalog Server. This server is usually the first Domain Controller to be set up in a forest. The GC contains information about all the objects in the directory and allows users and administrators to find the information they need regardless of the domain that contains this data.

This technology allows users of a computer network to work using personalized user and password entries. It doesn't matter if the user decides to use another computer, their personal settings and files can be accessed, as long as these machines are within the same domain controlled by a server.

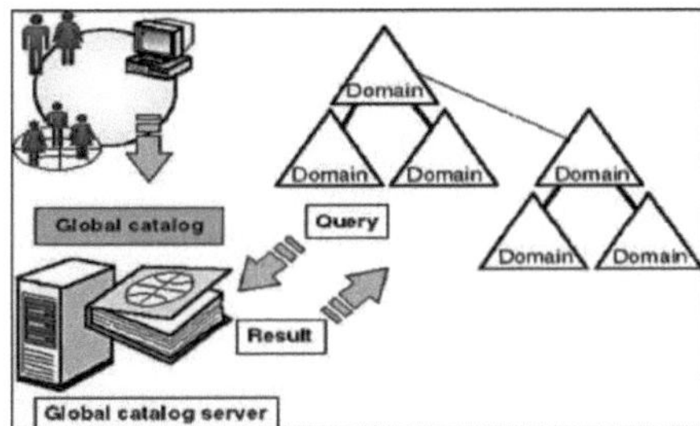

Figure 1.13 Global Catalog

Source: Nuno Alexandre Magalhaes Pereira; November 2004

1.14.3- Active Directory Development History

AD allows the creation of domains with millions of objects, making it possible to develop domains on a very large scale. The scenario of a worldwide company with just one domain is perfectly acceptable. In previous versions (e.g. Windows NT4), this was an impossible scenario mainly because the domains were much more limited in the number of users they supported, they didn't allow the creation of domain divisions with different administrative powers and also because Domain Controllers had no way of knowing how they were connected to each other, so they would perform the tasks of copying information concerning the domain in the same way, whether they were on the same local network, or connected via an extended network with much less capacity.

1.14.3.1- Windows 2000 Server

Microsoft Active Directory was launched in 1999 with Windows 2000 Server Edition. According to Microsoft (WINDOWS SERVER, 2014), historically, its main features were:

> Universal groups: For both security and distribution groups.

> Alignment of groups.

> Group conversion: Allows conversion between security and distribution groups.

> Security identifiers (SID).

If an Aoresta has the functional level of Windows 2000, these features will be available and if other domains are created on the network, the most advanced features will not be available on these domains, even if they are more recent versions.

1.14.3.2- Windows 2003 Server

AD was overhauled to extend its features and improve administration in Windows 2003 Server, when it underwent its biggest change. According to Microsoft (WINDOWS SERVER, 2014), in addition to the previous features, others were added such as:

> A domain management tool (Netdom.exe), which allows you to rename Domain Controllers.

> Date and time updates at session start: The IastLogonTimestamp attribute is updated with the last time a client logged on. This attribute is replicated in the domain.

> The ability to set the UserPassword attribute as the effective password on InetOrgPerson and user objects.

> The ability to redirect User and Machine Containers: by default, two known Containers are provided for home computers and user accounts, i.e. en = Computers, <root domain> and en = Users, <root domain> allowing a new Ioeal to be defined for these accounts.

> Authorization manager that stores authorization policies in AD.

> Restricted delegation: makes it possible for applications to take advantage of the secure delegation of user credentials through Kerberos-based authentication. It also makes it possible to restrict delegation to specific target services only.

> Selective authentication: allows you to specify the users and groups in a Trusted Forest that will be allowed to authenticate resource servers in a Trusted Forest. Domains created in an Aoresta at the Windows Server 2003 domain functional level will offer all the features of Windows 2000, plus the following additional features:

> Linked value replication, which improves the replication of changes in group associations.

> More efficient generation of complex replication topologies by the Knowledge Consistency Checker (KCC).

> Trust at the forest level, allowing easy sharing of organizations.

> Internal resources in multiple Aorestas.

1.14.3.3- Windows 2008 Server

Additional improvements have been included with Windows Server 2008. In addition to the functions already existing in Windows Server 2003, the following have been added:

> DFS (Distributed File System) with support for SYSVOL (Windows Server System Volume) volume replication;

> For domains based on DFS-type namespaces, support for access-based enumeration has been included, ensuring greater scalability (WINDOWS SERVER, 2008);

> AES 128 and AES 256 encryption in Kerberos authentication;

> Interactive Logon: Shows the time of the last successful logon and the number of failed attempts;

> Refined password rules: Allows rules to be determined for users and security groups within a domain (WINDOWS SERVER, 2009).

1.14.3.4- Windows 2008 R2

This version of Windows 2008, in addition to having all the native features, has an extra guarantee from the authentication mechanism, which works by grouping information about the type of logon method, allowing information to be extracted whenever a user tries to access any applications that recognize authorization based on a user's logon method.

1.14.3.5- Windows 2012 Server

This version has all the previous features, but adds improvements to Kerberos authentication, such as database compression.

1.14.3.6- Windows 2012 R2

This version created the siloed authentication policy in the forest, allowing you to create a relationship between users, services and computers, for the purposes of classifying accounts or isolating authentication.

1.14.4- Active Directory Infrastructure and Hierarchy

The AD Directory Service is subdivided into two structures, the logical structure and the physical structure. A basic knowledge of the structure of AD is important because it will help you understand how it works. Below, Rover Marinho[4] is an Active Directory expert and helps us to better understand the structure and hierarchy of AD.

1.14.4.1- - Active Directory Logical Structure

The logical structure of AD consists of Objects, Organizational Units (OU), Domains, Domain Trees and Forests. We use the logical structure of AD to be able to manage objects within the organization. AD physically also has a database, this database is known as **NTDS.dit** and is located in the **%SystemRoot%\NTDS\ntds.dit** folder in a default AD installation.

This directory, called NTDS, only exists on servers that are Domain Controllers (DC).

1.14.4.1.1 - Objects

They are the most basic components of the logical structure and represent users, computers and printers. Other objects can be created, but we'll just stick to these for now.

1.14.4.1.2 - Organizational Units

Urn OU is a *container* object used to organize other objects. It can be organized in various ways;

• Geographic - Where the ORs represent states or cities in your physical structure. Example: OU LAD - OU HLA

• Sectoral - Where the OUs represent sectors of the company's physical structure, by business units. Example: Administrative OU - Production OU

• Departmental - Where OUs represent sectors of the company's physical structure by department. Example: OR HR - OR DP - OR Boiler Room

• Hybrid - A model where all the above models can interact. An example is shown in the figure below.

---

4 Rover Marinho - Has been working in the infrastructure market since 1998, specializing in Active Directory, Exchange and Microsoft infrastructure products. He is MCP, MCSA, MCSE, MCTS, MCITP, MCT and MVP certified in Directory Services. http://www.linhadecodigo.com.br/windowsserver.aspx. Last accessed November 2016.

lifemotion.local
  Builtin
  Computers
  Domain Controllers
  ForeignSecurityPrincipals
  Managed Service Accounts
  Users
  lsd
    Administrativo
      RH
      DP
    Producao
      Caldeira

Figure 1.14 NTDS.dit to be replicated

Source: linhadecodigo.com.br/windowsserver.aspx

1.14.4.1.3 - Domains

0 domain is the most important structure in Active Directory and has two main functions:

❖ They close an administrative boundary to objects. "Whoever is outside does not enter, whoever is inside does not leave". Of course, this rule can be altered by entry and exit permissions, such as relationships of trust.

❖ They manage the security of accounts and resources within Active Directory.

Remember that Active Directory domains share:

❖ The same **Ntds.dit** database for each Domain Controller within this domain.

❖ Safety directives.

❖ Relationships of trust with other domains.

Trust relationships do not compromise security. They are only implemented to enhance the permissibility of access to resources. Access to resources should only be granted by administrators. This is why you should avoid granting any User or Authenticated User access to resources. Once trust relationships are established, everyone within the trust domains will have access to their resources as well. Desmond, B., 2013.

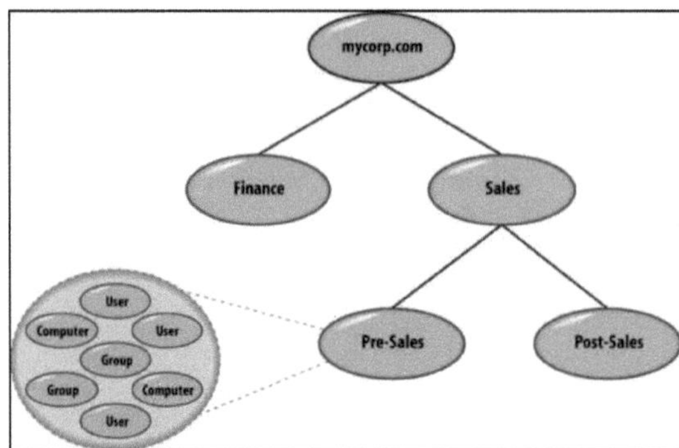

Figure 1.15 Object hierarchy

Source: Desmond, B., 2013.

1.14.4.1.4   - Domain Trees

When we need to create a second domain due to changes in the security process, we have what we call child domains. When we have a parent domain with its child domains, we call them a domain tree, because they share the same DNS suffix but in a hierarchical distribution. Below is an example to illustrate our explanation.

We have created the fao.org domain as shown in Figure 1.16, so that we can configure security directives. At some point we need to create a new domain, which has access to the resources of the fao.org domain, but has its own security needs, Figure 1.17.

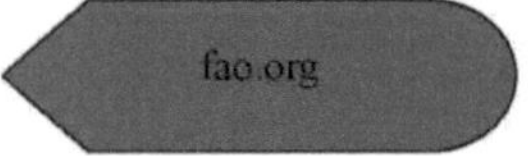

Figure 1.16 Single Domain

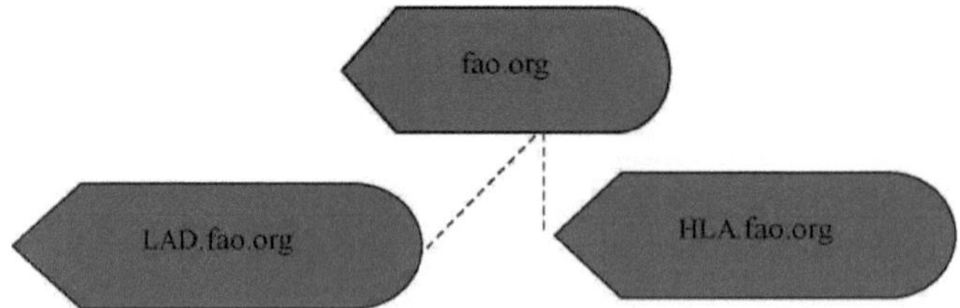

Figure 1.17 - Domain Tree

According to the figures above, we can see that when we have a child domain, we are immediately linked to a parent domain, and this hierarchical division of names is called a Domain Tree.

1.14.4.1.5   - Forests

The first domain of a forest is called the *Root Domain* and the forest is named after this domain. The forest can be made up of a single domain or it can be divided into several trees within the same forest.

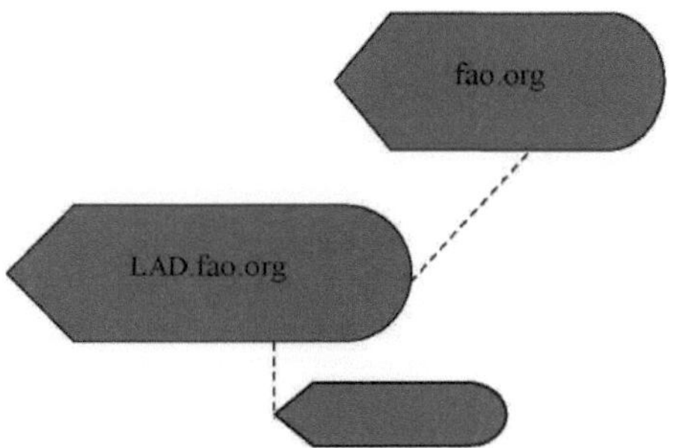

Figure 1.18 Forest Root Domain

1.14.5 - Physical Structure of Active Directory

When we talk about the physical structure of Active Directory, a few terms are used. The physical structure of AD consists of *Domain Controllers* and *Sites*. The physical structure of AD is totally independent of its logical structure. The physical structure is responsible for optimizing network traffic.

1.14.5.1 - Domain Controllers

At the beginning of this section we focused on trying to understand AD, now we're going to show and try to understand how Active Directory works in Domain Controllers (DC).

A Domain Controller has the function of running Active Directory and also storing the Active Directory database and replicating this database with other DCs. When we talk about Domain Trees or even Forests, it's worth remembering that a DC can only support a single domain. In order to create high availability for Active Directory, we can have more than one DC. For example, if we have two DCs, the Active Directory base will be replicated identically for both DCs. The Active Directory base, NTDS.dit, is divided into partitions, as shown in the figure below. These partitions form the NTDS.dit file, which is replicated between each of the DC's in your domain, consequently the file is replicated for each DC, having all the DC's Synchronized we will then have a healthy Active Directory.

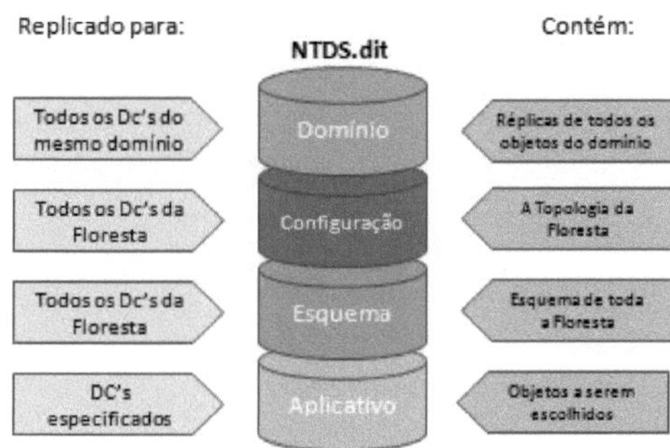

Figure 1.19 NTDS.dit partitions

Source: linhadecodigo.com.br/windowsserver.aspx

1.14.5.2 Replication

The process of transferring AD information between Domain Controllers in a forest in order to maintain homogeneity is called replication. Replication takes place periodically. Information about defined Sites (as we have seen, these are structures that define the interconnections between the machines in a domain) is used to manage the way in which replication takes place. Replication between controllers in the same Site happens more often than between controllers in different Sites.

Between Domain Controllers within the same Site, a program called KCC (Knowledge Consistency Checker) runs periodically and draws up a topology for replicating information efficiently.

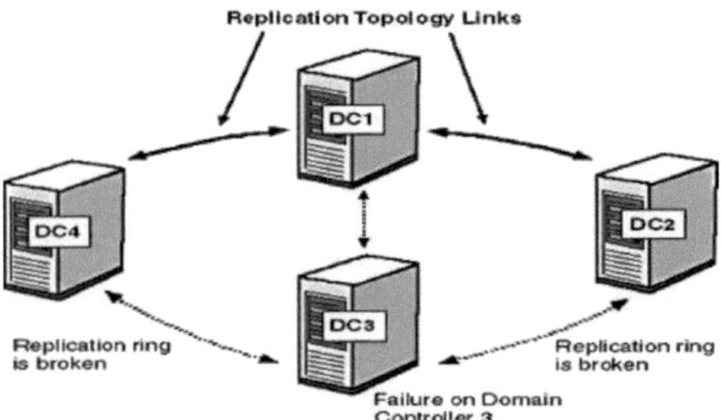

Figure 1.20 Replication topology

Source: Nuno Alexandre Magalhaes Pereira; November 2004

1.14.5.3   - Sites

Sites are used to organize the DC's replication lactation within the same site, as well as to ensure that the DC's of that particular site do not use the replication link unnecessarily. By organizing Active Directory sites, we can limit a certain group of computers to establishing contact with their Head Office, or vice versa, only at off-peak times; this concept is called replication scheduling. AD sites are used to ensure that a given *range* or *ranges* are separated by physical distances, but that the data from the DCs is replicated continuously or at pre-scheduled times, so that DCs are kept up to date even over long distances.

CHAPTER 2- METHODOLOGY

2.1 - Approach to methodology

2.1.1 Field of study

The FAO (Food and Agriculture Organization of the United Nations) is a Specialized Agency of the United Nations with its field of action on issues of Land, Agriculture and Food and Nutritional Security through programmes and projects designed in partnership with the Angolan government. Its representative offices are in Luanda and it operates on the ground in the interior of the country, where it has another office in the province of Huila, which serves the southern region of the country.

The case study was developed based on the FAO's need to consolidate two Active Directory domains located in different geographical areas. One located in the central offices in Luanda and the other in the sub-office in the province of Huila. We used the following methods to carry out this project:

> Research into monographs related to the topic.

> Discussions with colleagues from the Technical University of Angola.

> Search for books related to the topic.

> Visits to specialized websites and blogs on AD issues.

> Use of virtualization applications for simulations and other Microsoft tools for migrating and managing objects within AD.

2.2 - Current AD Diagnosis

The current AD structure at the FAO consists of two completely separate domains and forests in separate geographical locations, as mentioned above. When staff move from one office to another, they have different credentials as if they were another user. User group administration policies are not well defined. Configuring user properties or other objects manually is time-consuming and error-prone. In other words, performing day-to-day operations for both the network administrator and the users takes some time and effort. Figure 2.1 below illustrates the logical structure of the FAO's current AD.

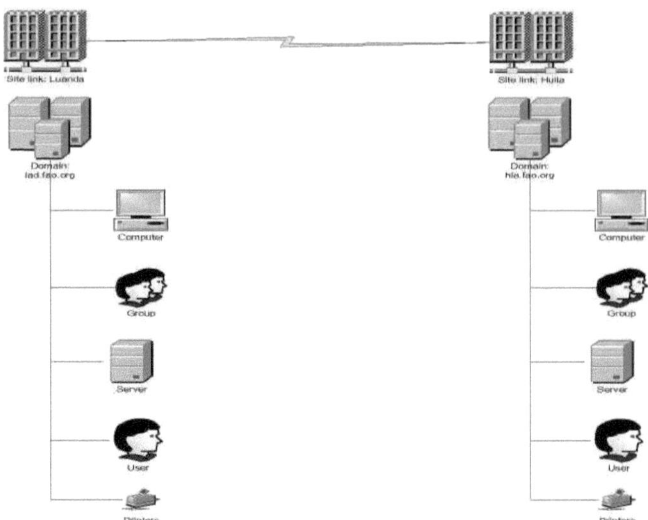

Figure 2.1 - Active Directory logic diagram

Although the domains are separate and not part of the same forest, it is possible to connect via *remote desktop connection* through the institution's WAN VPN, but the user's own PC may only belong to one of the domains. In order for them to access and gain access to all the network resources from either office, they will need to have both domains in the same forest. This is the ideal scenario, that the entire institution has just one forest housing several organizational units.

2.2.1 Restructuring Active Directory

Since the main objective of our work is to implement consolidated AD, it involves restructuring. Restructuring involves migrating resources between Active Directory domains in the same forest or in different forests. This restructuring was carried out using the mechanism for migrating objects between various OUs within AD. The use of the Active Directory Migration Tool (ADMT) to perform object migrations and security conversions is necessary so that users can maintain access to network resources during the migration process.

2.2.2 Methodological implementation

In order to be able to implement the project in practice, we used the machine virtualization method by installing VMware Workstation ver.10 on an HP ProBook Laptop with a i5@2.40 GHz x64-based processor, with original memory of 4.0 GB, which during the tests proved to be insufficient, forcing us to buy another 4.0 GB and expand the memory up to 8.0 GB. Windows Server 2012 R2 virtual machines were then deployed on vmware.

It is important to mention that due to the low hardware capacity of our host machine, it was not possible to implement other service servers. That's why we're only focusing on the services that are essentially related to our case study.

2.2.3 VMware workstation for Windows

VMware Workstation is currently used as the standard in the virtualization industry. Many IT professionals, application developers and companies use VMware Workstation Pro and VMware Workstation Player because they are faster, more productive and more secure. Both allow the user to run multiple operating systems including Linux and Windows simultaneously as virtual machines on a single PC. What's more, vmware is very easy to use and doesn't require much IT experience.

2.2.4 Windows Server 2012 R2 and Active Directory

They were deployed on the VMware workstation. The operating system was installed on servers that were later upgraded to Domain Controllers.

It's important to note that before starting any installation, migration or restructuring step, the IT professional should make a backup of the entire system so that they can be in a position to return to the original form if the process doesn't go smoothly. In our simulation case, this wasn't necessary because we were installing completely new services.

The roles needed to manage resources such as DNS, DHCP and AD were added to the servers, as well as other functionalities. The Active Directory Users and Computers tool was successfully added and made it possible to insert Users, define group policies (GPO), etc.

2.2.5 The Active Directory Migration Tool

The Active Directory Migration Tool (ADMT) is a Microsoft tool designed to migrate users, groups, autonomous or managed service accounts and computers between Active Directory domains in different forests (inter-forest migration) or between Active Directory domains in the same forest (intra-forest migration). This tool was used to restructure and migrate objects between ADs.

2.3 - The Network Topology and the Equipment Used

When we talk about a client/server network, it is necessary to take into account the types of equipment to be used on the network because a **Client-Server** network is a computing model that separates clients and servers, but they are interconnected through a physical medium. Although both machines are PCs with the same basic architecture, client and server computers usually have different hardware and software configurations. The network services are located on the server and each client can send data requests to one of the connected servers and wait for a response. In turn, any of the available servers can accept these requests, process them and return the result to the client.

The physical topology of the FAO office network in Angola is as follows:

Each office or *site* uses the same standardized configuration to simplify both configuration and debugging.

The topology adopted was **Star Topology** because it facilitates system maintenance and allows the problem to be detected more easily in the event of a fault. The Administration Subsystem consists of patch panels and patch cords that allow different services to be assigned to different sockets, such as voice and video. The computers are connected via UTP cat 6 twisted pair cables via RJ-45 sockets. The network application is Gigabit Ethernet 100/1000 Mbps.

Each firewall connects to a so-called "security switch" which serves as a demarcation point between the office and the WAN providers and between the security devices and other network devices such as switches and wireless devices such as WAPs. All *firewalls* and security switches are configured in the same way, using the same ports. The *firewall* and security switch are pre-configured with double cables and different colors to reduce the possibility of connectivity problems due to cable issues.

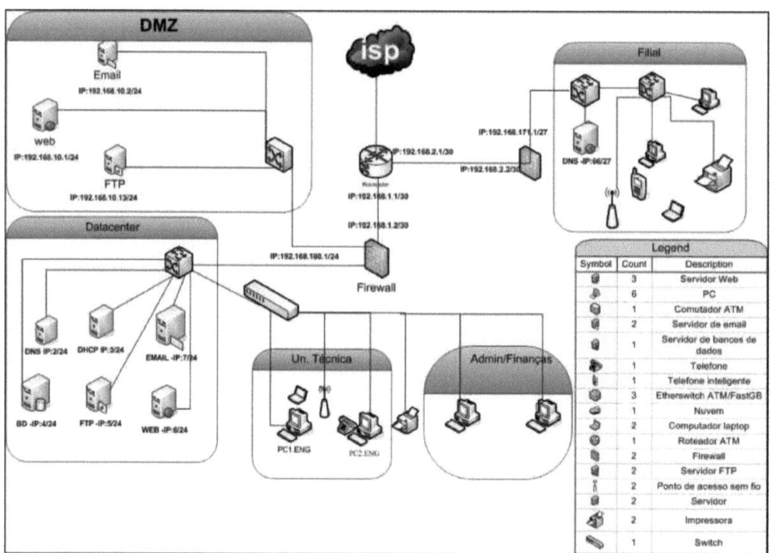

Legend		
Symbol	Count	Description
	3	Servidor Web
	6	PC
	1	Comutador ATM
	2	Servidor de email
	1	Servidor de bancos de dados
	1	Telefone
	1	Telefone inteligente
	3	Etherswitch ATM/FastGB
	1	Nuvem
	2	Computador laptop
	1	Roteador ATM
	2	Firewall
	2	Servidor FTP
	2	Ponto de acesso sem fio
	2	Servidor
	2	Impressora
	1	Switch

Figure 2.2 Current network logic diagram

The following devices are operating on the network:

Catalyst 2960 switch: 48-port switch with a speed of 100/1000 Mbps serves as a central point, allowing all points to communicate with each other, belonging to the link layer of the TCP/IP model.

Cisco 1900 series router: its function is to interconnect disparate networks by requesting packet traffic on the network. The 1900 series provides highly secure, high-performance connectivity with multi-service integration that can transform the workplace with a wide range of services, advanced media support and operational excellence. In the network it acts as a gateway to the WAN with VPN, to the Intranet and VoIP channel.

❖ **Juniper SG5:** router (layer 3) acts as a gateway and firewall between the three internal networks (TRUST, GUEST, DMZ) and the two external networks (UNTRUST links 1 and 2).

❖ **Netgear Prosafe GSM7248 security switch**: has configured VLANs (only at the head office) which also serve as a demarcation point between the office and the WAN providers and between the security devices and others such as switches and wireless devices.

❖ **EXinda Switch** - for network optimization, bandwidth monitoring and control.

❖ **Dell WAP:** Wireless access point for visitors. Station in the network DMZ.

❖ **Dell 540 servers:** their function is to make services available to other computers on the network.

❖ **IP PBX: is** responsible for managing and transforming the network into a telephony center, i.e. an **IP PBX** is a telephone exchange that allows internal communication (through extensions) and facilitates external communication (fixed telephone lines), managing calls, making communication more reliable and efficient, as it provides total confidentiality between calls.

❖ **HP Elite Pro 800 computers:** will allow user interaction with the system. These computers are Gigabit Ethernet, which allows them to communicate on the network with greater speed. They have a 3.0 GHz Intel Core Dual i5 processor and 4.00 GB of memory.

2.3.1 - Services available on the network

In a client/server network, it is imperative to have the services available on the network, taking into account the number of users and the workflow. The following services are available:

❖ **DNS** (Domain Name System): provides name resolution for TCP/IP-based networks, i.e. it enables users of client computers to use names, rather than numerical IP addresses, to identify remote hosts. The current domain name is ao.fao.org. Once our solution has been implemented, each site will be assigned a prefix indicating the site plus the main domain, e.g. lad. faoh.faol.com for the Luanda office.

❖ **AD** (Active Directory): Domain Controller authenticates and authorizes all users and computers in the Domain.

❖ **DHCP (Dynamic Host Configuration Protocol) is a** service that allows terminals to be configured by dynamically assigning IP addresses, subnet masks and gateways.

❖ **FTP (File Transfer Protocol):** the service that gives users access to the file server via the file transfer protocol.

❖ **Database:** the service that manipulates information contained in the database. This is where the SQL Server application will be installed. SQL Server is software that allows you to manage a database.

❖ **Firewall:** its function is to regulate data traffic between different networks and prevent harmful or unauthorized access to the network. The *firewall* uses one or more methods to control the traffic circulating on the network, such as: packet filtering, proxy services and *statefull inspection.*

❖ **Electronic Mail Server:** responsible for processing and delivering messages electronically.

2.3.2 Security

Institutions that are completely dependent on Information and Communication Technology systems have to take into account the security of these systems. The security level of a network or system consists of defining the logical and physical resources that need to be protected.

2.3.3 Physical Security

Physical security is the set of methods used to maintain the integrity, confidentiality and availability of information in the institution. Without physical security, access by an unauthorized person to a computer can result in the disclosure of information, alteration of information and also the destruction of information. The FAO has security measures in place, such as access to facilities only for well-identified and accredited persons. There is a server room with access restricted to the network administrator.

2.3.4 Logical Security

Logical security is the way in which the system is protected at the operating system and application level. It is usually thought of as protection against attacks, but it also means system protection against unintentional errors, such as additional removal of important system or application files, occasional virus threats, remote network access, outdated backups, password breaches, hardware or software errors, processing failures, communication errors or bugs in programs, incorrect data entry, incorrect disk mounting or loss of a disk, etc.

The practice at the institution is that only employees with a valid contract have access to a computer. Access to both systems and PCs is only valid for the duration of the contract. Each user is clearly identified and grouped in their Organizational Unit in Active Directory, meaning that they only have access to certain information in the system.

2.3.5 Network addressing

Figures 2.1 and 2.3 below, the IP address and distribution tables, define how IP addresses will be made available on the network. All servers and peripheral devices such as *routers, Jirewalls and switches* are assigned fixed IPs, while PCs receive dynamic IPs from the DHCP service.

	Network End	Home	Final	Mascara
IP/Public	192.168.1.0	192.168.1.1/30	192.168.1.2/30	255.255.255.254
IP/Private	192.160.10.0/24	192.168.10.1/24	192.168.10.25/24	255.255.255.0

Table 2.1: Addressing table

CHAPTER 3 - RESULTS

In this section, we present what has been achieved as a result of the application of studies and research concerning the implementation of the restructuring of Active Directory and its consolidation, starting with the presentation of the proposed logical diagram and then the installation of the servers and configuration of the services, primarily Active Directory Domain Services (AD DS).

3.1 Logic diagram of the proposed new AD

The restructuring of the FAO's AD DS environment will be carried out in order to optimize the arrangement of elements within the logical structure of the Active Directory - allowing for greater versatility and ease of administration of the entire network. Figure 3.1 below shows the logical diagram proposed for the FAO's new consolidated Active Directory.

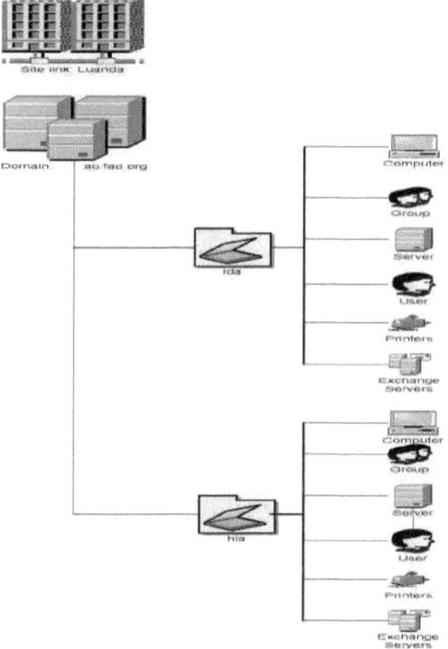

Figure 3.1 Proposed diagram for the new consolidated AD

The new restructured AD will work in a consolidated way, i.e. the two previously separate domains, each belonging to its own forest, will now belong to the same Forest domain even though they are still in different geographical locations. As figure 3.1 illustrates, the LAD.fao.org and HLA.fao.org domains are unified within the same Forest, but are separate OUs. After the migration and consolidation process, certain common process policies will have to be implemented in order to allow users to move between the two *sites* (LAD and HLA), i.e. when a user moves from one site to the other, they will have access to corporate network resources in the same way without having to configure a process each time they move.

3.2 Deployment of domain servers and AD DS configuration

The following figures illustrate the deployment of the servers from their configuration to their promotion with domain controllers. They will also show how ADMT v32 works when migrating objects between domain forests and from domain to domain. For convenience and ease of reading this document, only the most demonstrative images of the process will be shown. Other demonstrations will be made in practice during the presentation of the work to avoid the document becoming full of pages with images of no technical relevance.

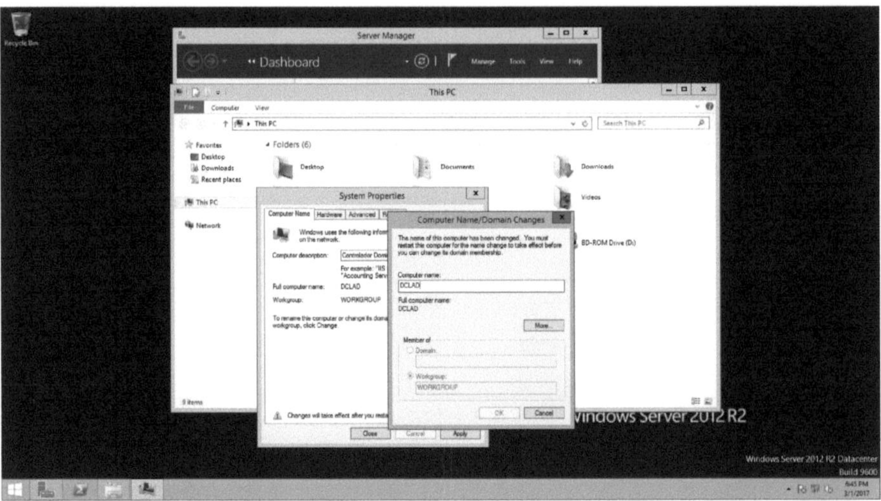

Figure 3.2 Preparing and configuring the servers - name assignment

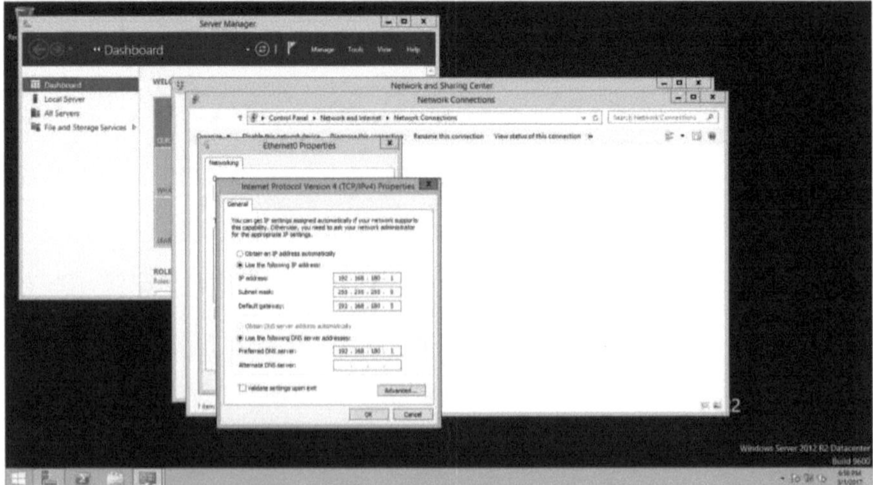

Figure 3.3 Preparing and configuring servers - assigning IP addresses

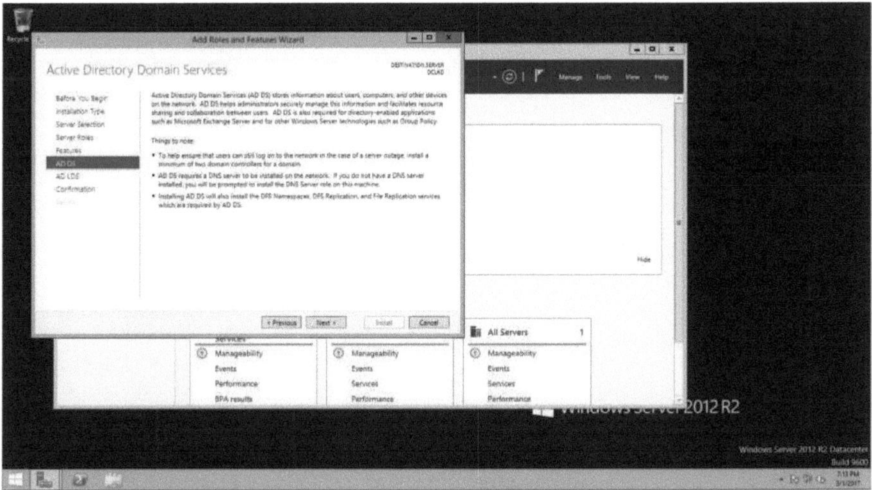

Figure 3.4 Promoting servers to DC domain controllers - adding AD DS

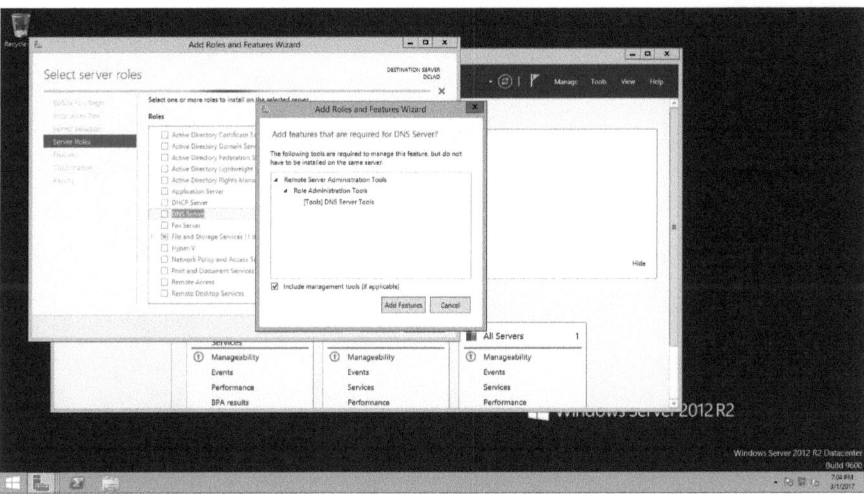

Figure 3.5 Promoting servers to domain controllers (DC) - adding DNS

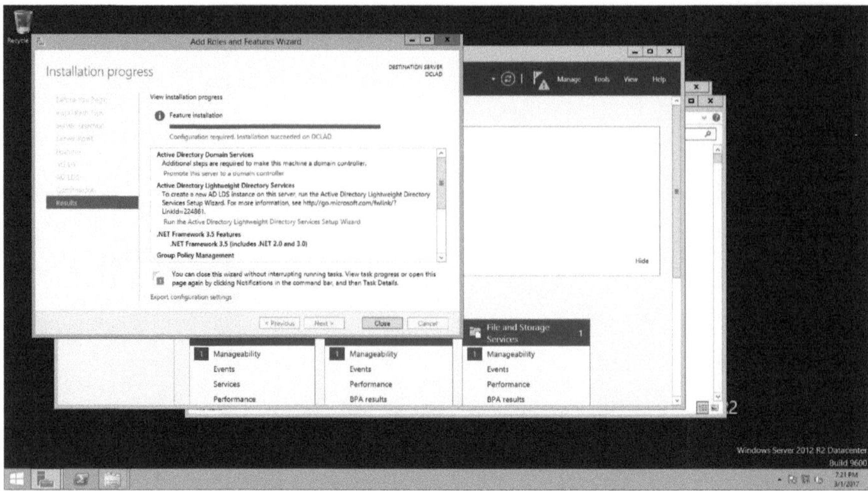

Figure 3.6 Promoting servers to domain controllers (DC) - installation progress

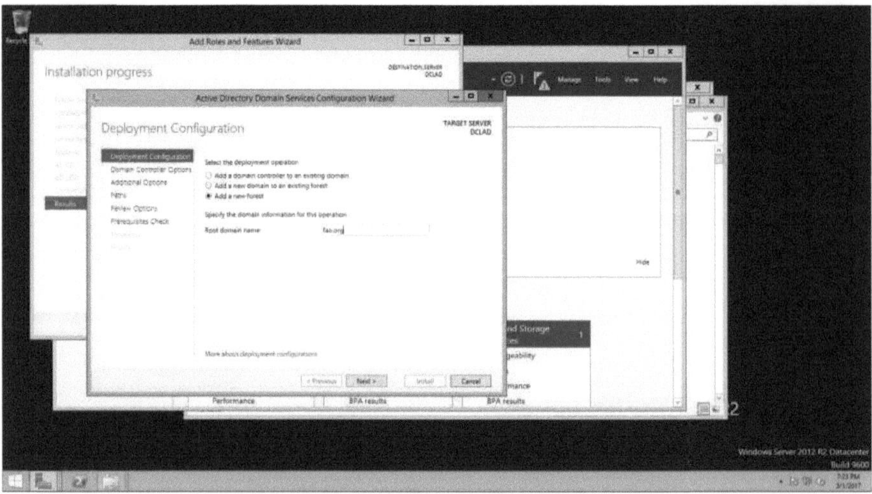

Figure 3.7 promoting servers to domain controllers (DC) - creating the domain root

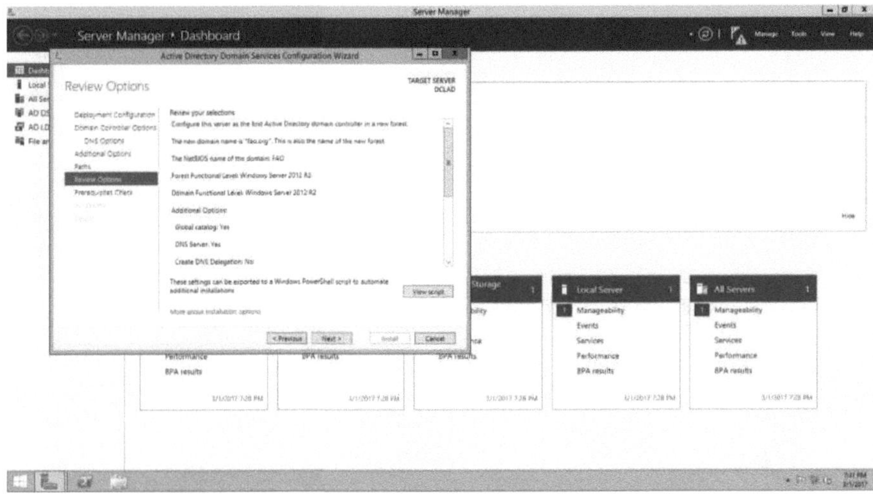

Figure 3.8 review of the options after creating the domain root

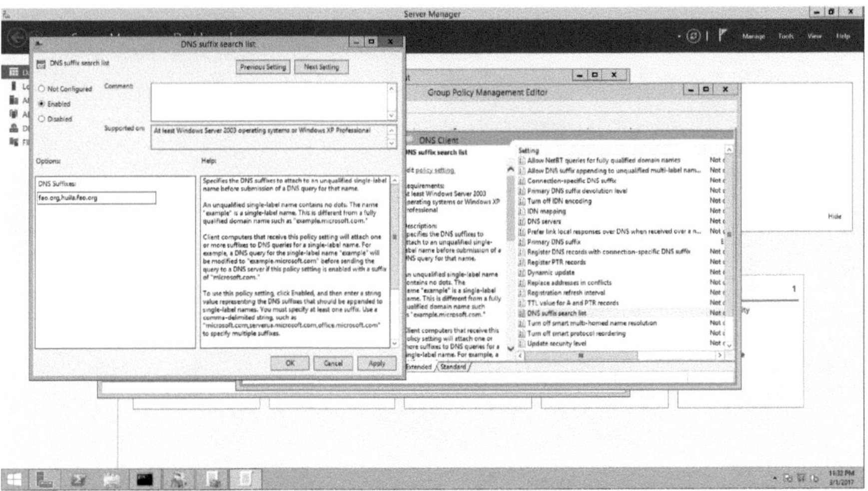

Figure 3.9 DNS configuration - assigning the primary DNS suffix

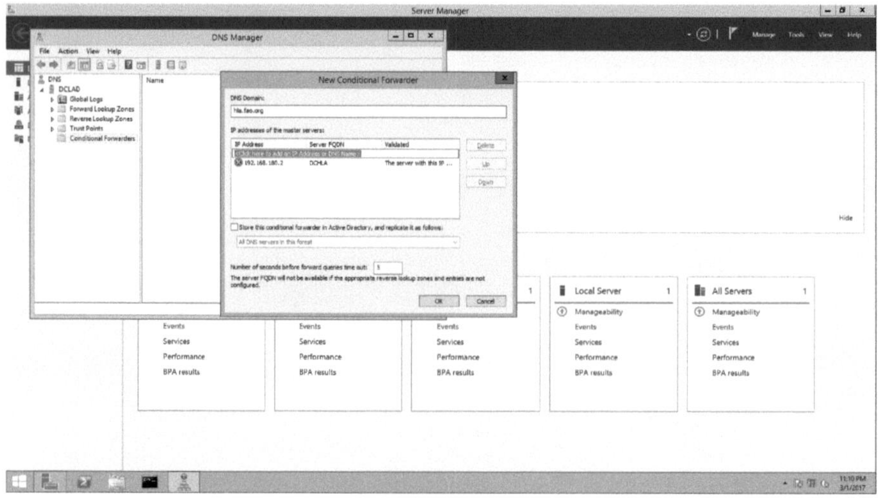

Figure 3.10 DNS configuration - reverse and forward zone configuration

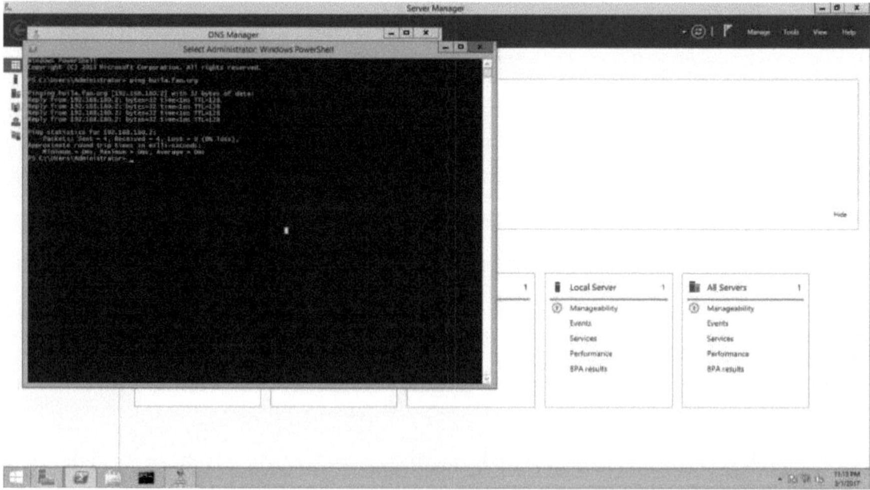

Figure 3.11 DNS configuration - inter-zone communication test

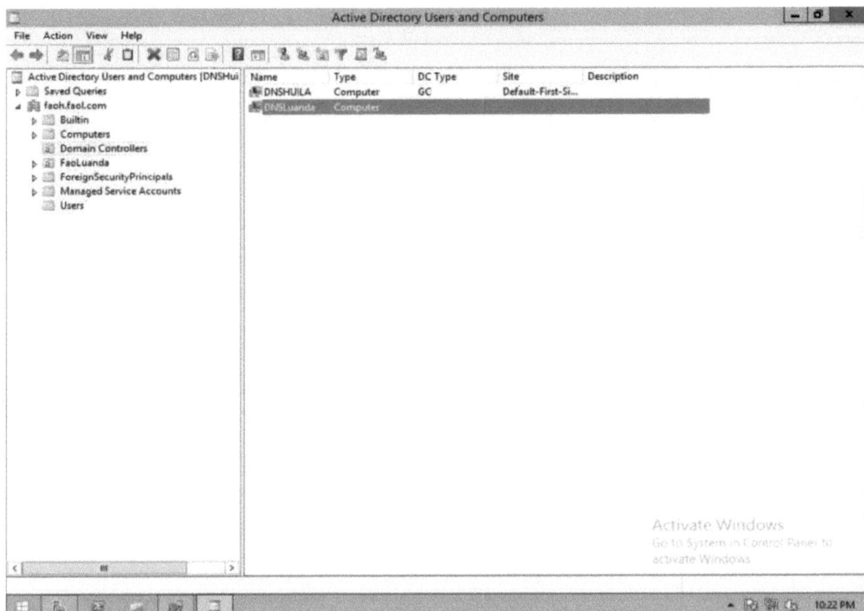

Figure 3.12 DNS configuration - servers added as DCs of the same domain

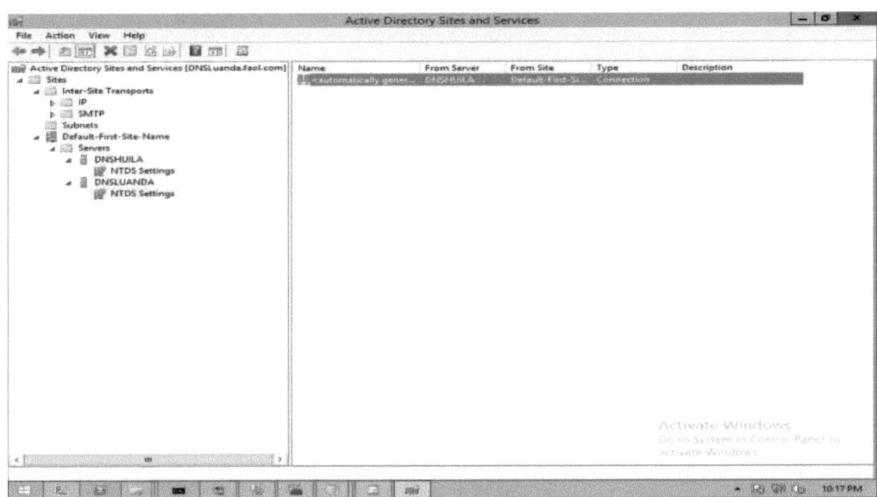

Figure 3.13 DNS of the two sites added to the same Domain Forest

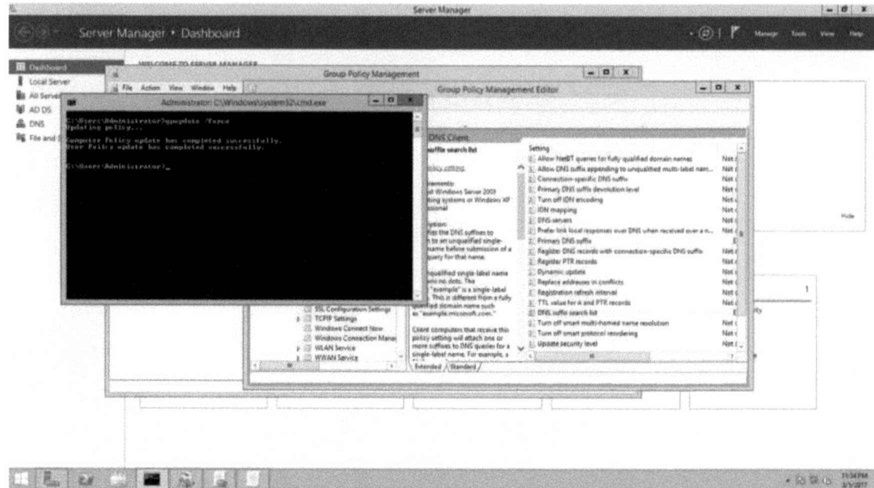

Figure 3.14 Group policy management in AD - application of the "gpupdate" commandlet

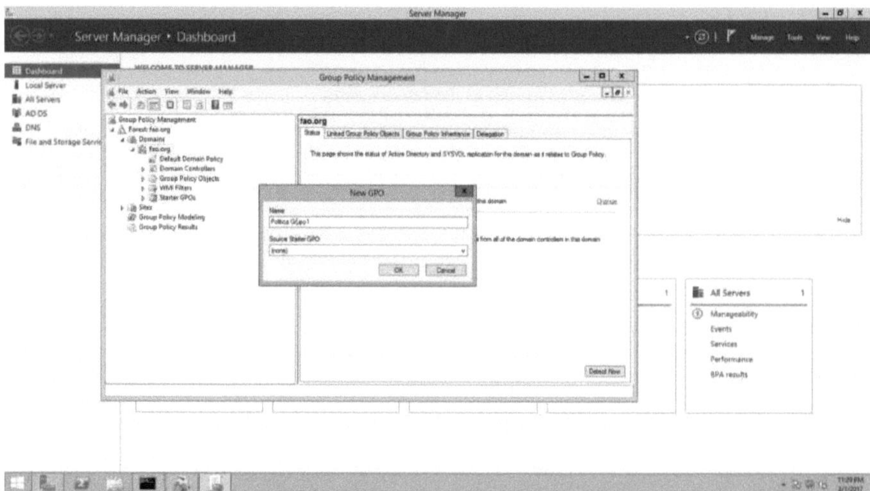

Figure 3.15 Group policy management in AD - new policy

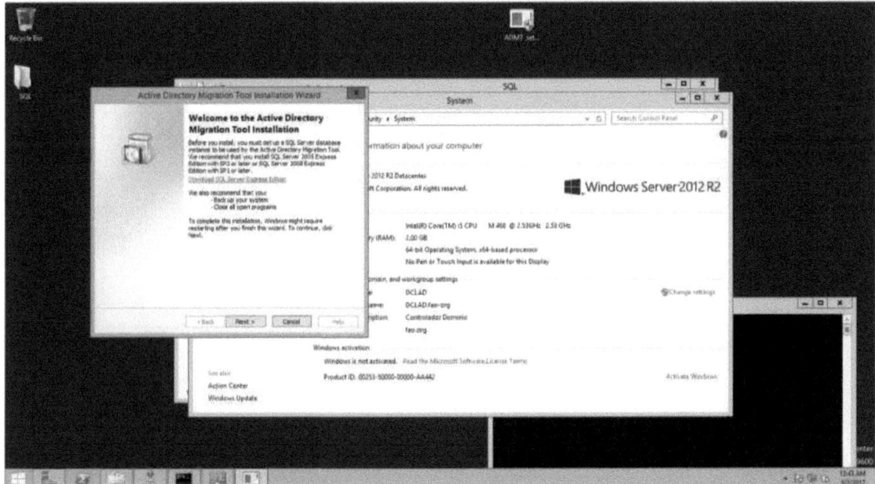

Figure 3.16 ADMT - installation of ADMT v3.2

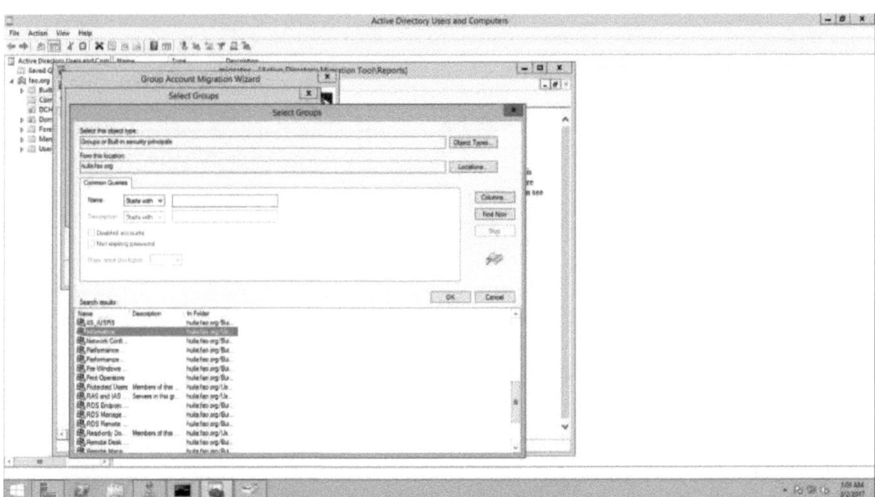

Figure 3.17 ADMT group account migration - group selection

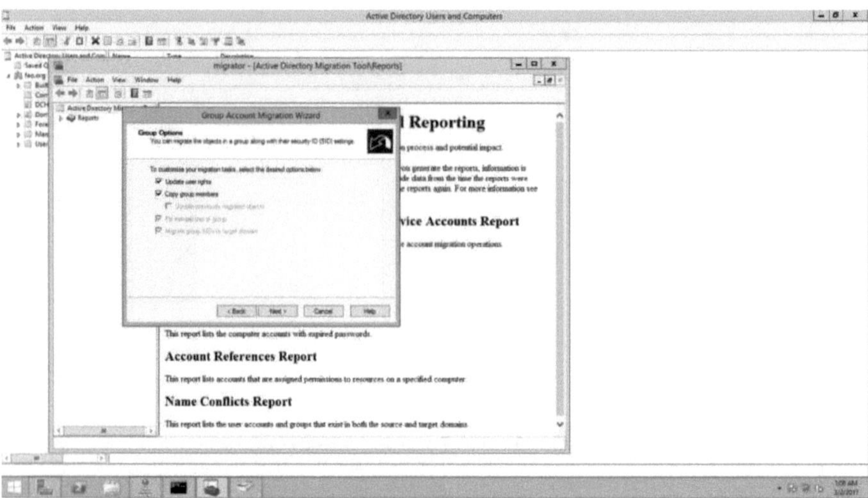

Figure 3.18 ADMT group account migration - group migration options

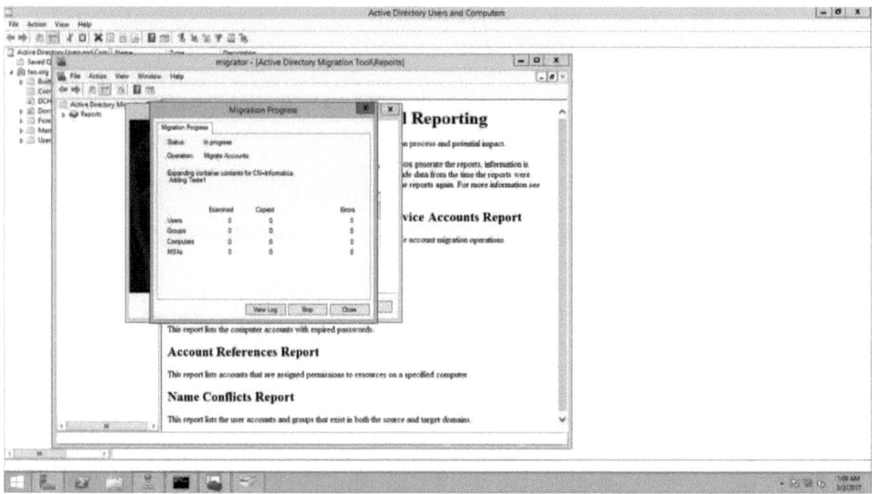

Figure 3.19 ADMT group account migration - observation of migration progress

3.3 Practical Guide to Implementing a Consolidated AD

Mitch Tulloch[5] , a well-known specialist in Windows Server administration and *cloud computing* technologies, has made some valuable contributions in the field of AD migration and consolidation, which we have transcribed here and leave as a recommendation for professionals in the field to be aware of what to do when thinking about restructuring or consolidating Active Directory domains and forests.

5http://www.windowsnetworking.com/articles-tutorials/windows-server-2012/active-directory-migration-considerations-part1.html. Last published and updated on October 7, 2014, accessed in July 2016.

1. The cost factor - A key factor to consider when thinking about restructuring or consolidating domains is the financial cost involved. You can greatly simplify Active Directory administration within an organization by consolidating all of its various domains into a single new domain. However, the cost of doing this can be so high that it constitutes an unacceptable investment for the company. The reason for this is that Active Directory consolidation/restructuring can be detrimental in many ways to the day-to-day IT operations of the organization. Some examples of the way in which domain consolidation/restructuring can disrupt day-to-day operations include o the time and effort required to test the effects of this task on the following: Administration of users, groups, computers and printers; Deployment, management and maintenance of client computers; Authentication, authorization and access to shared folders, shared printers and other network resources; Authentication, authorization and access to server applications and services; Delegation of authority to perform Active Directory administration; The amount of WAN traffic used for Active Directory replication between *sites* in the same domain; and many other factors. Of course, having only a single domain in the forest has its own benefits, including: More centralized management and monitoring of Active Directory and the application server; Fewer domain controllers to manage within your environment; Easier resolution of Active Directory replication problems and trust issues; Fewer problems with inconsistencies in the way Group Policy is configured and applied; Simplified implementation and management of "bring your own device" (BYOD); Simplified authentication and access control when services are provided in the Cloud; Easier forest/domain consolidation in the future, in the event of corporate mergers or acquisitions. However, the road to get there (to have just a single domain in your Forest) can be so costly in terms of time and effort (and therefore money) that it may not be worth your organization's while to restructure/consolidate all existing Active Directory domains. In the end, you should carefully consider the cost before embarking on such a project - especially if you're going to hire external consultants to do the work.

2. Mitigating the cost factor; one way to mitigate the cost involved in Active Directory restructuring / consolidation projects is to include them as part of a larger infrastructure modernization project. For example, let's say that a company's IT infrastructure is still traditional/conventional with Asico servers in their *datacenters*. Now you want to completely modernize your infrastructure by virtualizing local server workloads and moving some of those workloads to the cloud. You can see some of the benefits that an organization can get from hybrid computing, such as resource *pooling*, elasticity, continuous availability, and so on. If the decision has been made to modernize the infrastructure, now is probably the time to include domain restructuring/consolidation as part of the overall infrastructure improvement project. Another good way to mitigate the cost involved in Active Directory restructuring / consolidation is to perform these tasks when you are launching a new server operating system in your organization. For example, if you're migrating from Windows Server 2003 to Windows Server 2012 R2, you might want to include domain restructuring / consolidation as a component of your overall server migration plan. Another cost-effective reason for carrying out Active Directory restructuring / consolidation is when you plan to modernize global business processes in order to ensure that your company remains competitive in the marketplace. If you're going to spend tens of millions of dollars to modernize your facilities and business processes, then taking a few more

millions to make your Active Directory infrastructure more accessible for the implementation of Cloud solutions can be much more attractive from a cost/benefit point of view.

3. Teamwork and a good migration plan: one important thing to remember, however, is that this task must be carried out by a multidisciplinary team. You need to get the entire IT management team on board and draw up a good Active Directory migration plan. This will ensure that solving an existing technical problem doesn't inadvertently create new problems, such as the *Helpdesk* being unable to cope with the volume of user complaints during the migration. Remember, frustrated users mean that the job isn't getting done and that there is, in the meantime, a loss of productivity, which can result in a loss of business. And IT's job is to be a business driver; IT doesn't exist in its own right or purpose.

4. Rollback: depending on the size and complexity of the Active Directory environment and the IT professional's own level of expertise (and self-confidence) in this area, they may or may not want to use ADMT to migrate or consolidate the Active Directory environment. If there is a lack of confidence and experience, external help can be involved, for example from Microsoft Consulting Services (MCS). On the other hand, even if you are fairly confident in your own technical ability and feel that you can handle things when something goes wrong, you may still want to choose not to use ADMT to carry out your migration. Why? Because ADMT's rollback functionality is not completely effective. Specifically, reversing migrations between forests is not possible with ADMT. Another limitation is ADMT's scalability. Let's say, for example, that you need to migrate 100,000 forest users from one domain to another. You can use ADTM to do this, but it will take some time. Given some of the limitations and especially the lack of secure rollback for migrations between Aorestas, if you need to perform a migration between Aorestas, you might want to consider using one of the Active Directory restructuring and migration offerings available commercially from other vendors such as Dell, which bought the Quest application two years ago. But can ADMT really cope with an increased migration volume of this order? Yes, as long as you're using Microsoft SQL Server instead of Microsoft SQL Server Express as your database migration engine. The full version of SQL Server can scale far beyond what the Express version is capable of, so if you're migrating hundreds of thousands of users, then you should definitely choose SQL Server to take advantage of the extra scalability.

5. Consider what to do first, consolidate or upgrade: let's suppose that the Active Directory Infrastructure consists of two Aorestas running Windows Server 2008 R2. The company's objective is to modernize and simplify its infrastructure to make it more powerful and easier to manage. To achieve this goal, you want to perform two tasks:

- Consolidate the two forests into a single forest.

- Upgrade your Domain Controllers (DC) to Windows Server 2012 R2.

The question you now face is this: should you start by consolidating the two Windows Server 2008 R2 Aorestas into a single Windows Server 2008 R2 Aoresta and then upgrade it to Windows Server 2012 R2 Active Directory? Or should you do it the other way around, for example, start by upgrading the Windows Server 2008 R2 Aorestas to o Windows Server 2012 R2 Active Directory and then consolidate the upgraded

Aorestas into a single Windows Server 2012R2 Aoresta?

In other words, what should you do first: consolidate your Aorestas or upgrade them to the latest versions of Active Directory? The answer is quite simple to deduce from the number of steps shown in the diagram below. In other words, you should start by consolidating one Forest into another and then upgrade the surviving Forests to a more up-to-date version of Active Directory.

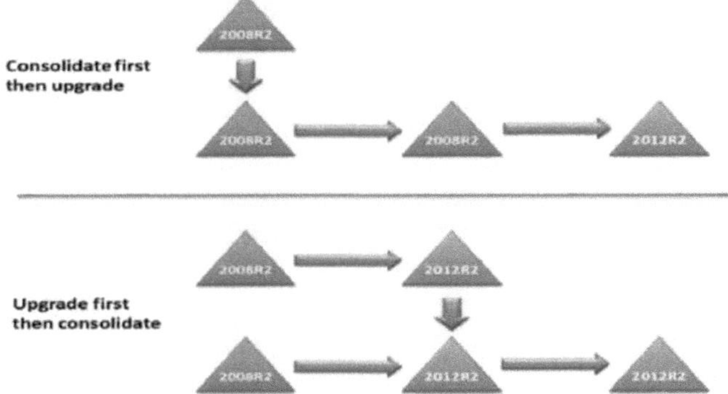

Figure 3.20 Consolidation versus Updating

Source: Mitch Tulloch, October 2014

CONCLUSION

The migration of objects and domains in Active Directory in Windows 2012 R2 proved to be a difficult task because it requires the professional in the field to have advanced knowledge of the tools inherent in the process, such as ADMT v3.2 for example, which allowed us to take advantage of the new resources provided by Active Directory. This new architecture brings a number of benefits, including the integration of the email system at corporate level, allowing users to share their schedules with other users globally, and access to the corporate management system is simplified through a single user password. On the other hand, and no less importantly, the maintenance of the local IT infrastructure is automated, improving resilience to disasters. In this chapter we have highlighted a small series of reflections that examine things that IT professionals should be aware of before restructuring or consolidating Active Directory domains and forests.

Knowledge of the Active Directory Migration Tool (ADMT) and how to use it is fundamental to any Active Directory migration process, including domain restructuring and consolidation. The ADMT (Active Directory Migration Tool) helped identify possible problems before starting the migration and made it easier to consolidate the two domains and convert them into Organizational units within the target Active Directory domain. However, using ADMT poses some challenges, especially for large companies that have to migrate more than a hundred users.

Active Directory Migration and/or Consolidation projects should not be considered trivial. There is a lot involved in the process, so the decision must be made taking into account all the aspects already mentioned here. The final decision must come from the top of the organization, but it must be cautious and prudent. It may not be necessary to consolidate the domains, so consider leaving them as they are!

RECOMMENDATIONS

The main focus of this work was the implementation of a Consolidated Domain and Forest Active Directory to optimize the arrangement of elements within the logical structure of the Active Directory, allowing for greater versatility and ease in the administration of the entire network. The next step would then be to migrate all these services to the Cloud where Users would have access to the organization's systems in a simplified way, accessing SharePoint so that they could share documents between the entire organization.

Before embarking on a consolidation project, the cost must be taken into account, especially if you are going to hire external consultants or even a third-party company to do the work.

One question that needs to be asked is what should be done first: consolidate existing Aorestas or upgrade them to newer versions of Active Directory? It is necessary to take into account which will take longer to carry out in addition to the cost, as has already been mentioned. You should start by consolidating the Aorestas within a single domain and then upgrade to a later version of Active Directory.

BIBLIOGRAPHICAL REFERENCES

Books:

ROSA, Antonio - Windows Server 2012, complete course. Ed 2013, FCA.

ROSA, Antonio - Windows Server 2008, complete course. Ed 2010, FCA.

BOAVIDA, Fernando | BERNARDES, Mario | VAPI, Pedro - Administraçao de Redes Informaticas. Ed 2011, FCA.

Gouveia, José | Magalhaes, Alberto-Computer Networks, complete course. Ed 2013, FCA.

BRIAN, Desmond, JOE, Richards, ROBBIE, Allen, ALISTAIR, G, LOWE, Norris, **Active Directory**, 5ª Edition, Editora-O'REILLY, 2013, USA.

HOLME, Dan - Configuring Windows Server 2008. Active Directory. MCTS 70-640 Exam Training Kit. Ed 2012, Bookman.

Sites/blogs:

https://www.manageengine.com/products/ad-manager/active-directory-management.html?ADMPID=%2015102&kw=Modify%20active%20directory%20users&adId={creative}⅛utm source=bing&utm medium=cpc&utm campaign=ADMP%20Search%20US&utm_term=Modify%20active%20directory%20user. Accessed June 2015

https://www.manageengine.com/products/ad-manager/active-directory-exchange-management.html, Accessed June 2015 https://blogs.technet.microsoft.com/brzad/2008/12/ll/conceitos-florestas-rvore-e-domnios/

Accessed June 2015 http://www.windowsnetworking.com/articles-tutorials/windows-server-2012/active-directory-migration-considerations-part1.html. Accessed July 2016 http://blogs.gartner.com/earl-perkins/2011/02/25/active-directory-consolidation-as-a-design-philosophy/ Accessed March 2016

http://www.linhadecodigo.com.br/windowsserver.aspx. Last accessed November 2016.

APPENDIX

I. Address distribution table

Name	IP/Public	Mascara
Router-Link-ISP	10.10.0.1	255.255.255.252
Firewall-	10.10.0.2	255.255.255.252
///// ///// ///// ///// /////	**IP/Private**	**Mascara**
Security switch	192.160.10.1	255.255.255.0
DNS-AD server	192. 160.10.2	255.255.255.0
DHCP server	192. 160.10.3	255.255.255.0
Database server	192. 160.10.4	255.255.255.0
Web server	192160.10.5	255.255.255.0
Mail server	192160.10.6	255.255.255.0
File Server	192160.10.7	255.255.255.0

Appendix I: IP address distribution

II. Physical Network Diagram

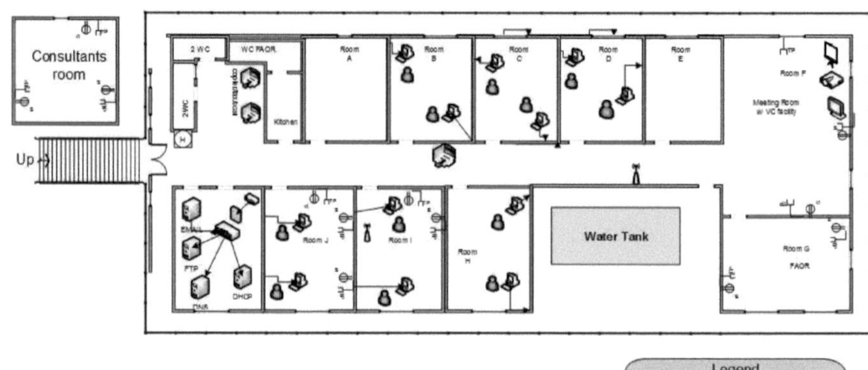

Roofsurface: 476 m²
Building surface: 335 m²

3 offices 4x5,5= 66 m²
1 office 4,5x5,5= 24,75 m²
5 offices 4x4,5= 90 m²
1 meeting room 6x12 to be divided for FAOR Room = 72 m²
1 room 2x4,5= 9 m²
2 toilets, one privative to be build FAOR

Office superficie= 261,75 m²

Legend		
Symbol	Count	Description
	3	Multi-function device
	2	Wireless access point
	1	LCD monitor
	1	Screen
	1	CRT projector
	5	Exchange Server
	1	Hub
	1	Firewall
	1	Roteador
	12	PC
	12	Usuário

Appendix II: Physical diagram of the network

III. Financial Cost Table

MANUFACTURER	DESCRIPTION	QUANTITY	PRICE UNIT.KZ	TOTAL KZ
Cisco	Cisco 3960 ATM router	1	90.000,00	90.000,00
Catalyst	Switch 2960	1	66.000,00	66.000,00
Junniper	SG5 gateway/firewall	1	83.490,00	83.490,00
Netgear	Prosate GSM7248 security switch	1	104.775,00	104.775,00
EXinda	Switch network traffic analysis & optimization	1	40.000,00	40.000,00
Dell	Poweredge r730 Intel® Xeon® E5-2640 v4 2.4GHz,25M. 32GB RDIMM	1	800.250,00	800.250,00
Sub-Total				1.184.515
Project Manager	Project leader/manager	1	170.041,09	170.041,09

Administrator Systems	Infrastructure Specialist	2	80.077,90	160.155,08
Sharepoint Administrator	Management Specialist SharePoint/ OneDrive	2	90.099,71	180.199,42
Database administrator	Database Specialist	1	70.000,00	70.000,00
Administrator Networks	Communication network specialist	1	70.087,03	70.087,03
Sub-Total				**497.482,62**
Microsoft	Windows Server 2012R2	1	115.335,00	115.335,00
Microsoft	SQL Server2012	1	165.000,00	165.000,00
Microsoft	Active Directory Migration Tool v3.2	1	Free tool	Free tool
Dell	Dell Migration Manager	U$12 for each user to be migrated.		
Sub-Total				**280.335,00**

They are: One Million, Nine Hundred and Sixty-Two Thousand, Three Hundred and Thirty-Three Kuanzas and Sixty-Two Cents.

Appendix III: Table of equipment, software and labor costs

In the previous chapters we looked at the financial costs involved when thinking about restructuring or consolidating domains. In this section we intend to present the comparative amounts that companies can spend to complete this task. Remember that the costs involved vary depending on the reality of each institution (e.g. its size). In this context, the table above illustrates the costs involved in *software*, equipment and labor, broken down by item. For those institutions like the one in our case study that already have all the equipment, they have only invested in the *software* and some network devices. The prices and quantities are for reference only, based on those prevailing on the local market as well as abroad. The equipment may also differ from that listed here.

I want morebooks!

Buy your books fast and straightforward online - at one of world's fastest growing online book stores! Environmentally sound due to Print-on-Demand technologies.

Buy your books online at
www.morebooks.shop

Kaufen Sie Ihre Bücher schnell und unkompliziert online – auf einer der am schnellsten wachsenden Buchhandelsplattformen weltweit! Dank Print-On-Demand umwelt- und ressourcenschonend produziert.

Bücher schneller online kaufen
www.morebooks.shop

info@omniscriptum.com
www.omniscriptum.com

Printed by Books on Demand GmbH, Norderstedt / Germany